D1502580

LIVING THE LORD'S PRAYER

LIVING THE LORD'S PRAYER

Our Power and Promise

Richard Andersen

Copyright © 1994 Concordia Publishing House
3558 S. Jefferson Avenue, St. Louis, MO 63118-3968
Manufactured in the United States of America

Library of Congress Cataloging-in-Publication Data.

Andersen, Richard, 1931–
    Living the Lord's prayer: our power and promise/ Richard
        Andersen.
        Includes bibliographical references.
        ISBN 0-570-04665-3:
        1. Lord's prayer—Meditations. 2. Christian life—Lutheran
    authors. I. Title.
    BV230.A64 1994
    226.9'606—dc20   94-12136
                                                            CIP

1 2 3 4 5 6 7 8 9 10   03 02 01 00 99 98 97 96 95 94

For the Rev. Harold Mitchell
and Director of Youth Ministries
Theo Olson,
who have accompanied me in these
prayerful wanderings,
and for Agnes Fraser, who encouraged me
in the project,
as well as for my grandchildren,
Michael, Erin, and Lauren Bova
as they make a
confession of
the Lord's Prayer
for the decades ahead.

CONTENTS

INTRODUCTION

The Church of the Pater Noster on Jerusalem's Mount of Olives is decorated with colorful tiles that portray the Lord's Prayer in 80 different languages, some well-known, others obscure. Similar to "mission and purpose" plaques in secular institutions, these 80 depictions tacitly proclaim that people everywhere are confessing themselves to be disciples of Jesus. Pilgrims from around the world seek out their language and have their picture taken, standing before this declarative prayer. Proudly they show them to friends back home. The photos announce not only the visitors' nationality but also their affirmation of the meaning behind the words. They confess the God whom Jesus addressed in the prayer, the heavenly Father, the one whose name is to be hallowed.

The Lord's Prayer (found in Matt. 6:9–13 and Luke 11:2–4) is definitely prayer. Yet it takes on the connotation of confession for several reasons. First of all, it was given by Jesus to His followers to identify them specifically as His disciples. It is, as Dr. Barclay declares, "specifically and definitely" a disciple's *prayer*. Yet, it also has the quality of a creed about it. The *Encyclopaedia Britannica* terms it a "unifying bond," this prayer of Jesus, that knits together believers and their Lord. Martin Luther, in his Large Catechism, says of the Apostles' Creed that it teaches "us all that we must expect and receive from God; in brief, it teaches us to know Him fully."[1] I submit that this aim is central to the Lord's Prayer as well.

Although Jesus denounced prayer when it resulted in mere recitation, He elevated it as a thing to be lived out. He told the woman of Samaria, "God is spirit, and His worshipers must worship in spirit and in truth" (John 4:24). Paul advised us, "Be joyful always; pray continually; give thanks in all circumstances, for this is God's will for you in Christ Jesus. Do not put out the Spirit's fire" (1 Thess. 5:16–19). Taken together, and from the Lord's own example, prayer is communication with God, yet it is also a declarative statement of faith—not something to be paraded, but something to be lived out in life, confessed by actions as well as words.

One professor of mine used to speak about the jewel that is the Lord's Prayer. He marveled at the church he had visited the Sunday before, where the clergyman, with eyes wide open, led the congregation not in praying the prayer but *confessing* it. Those who speed through a recitation of the prayer in no time and without thinking about its implications might try the wide-awake declaration the professor described. In fact, all of us might well consider the prayer as a creed and confess it openly by living it rather than simply reciting it, heaping up the "empty phrases" that Jesus denounced (Matt. 6:7 RSV).

To a large degree, confession is the purpose of the prayer. It identified the Twelve as followers of the One who originated the prayer. Other rabbis did the same thing, giving their disciples an identifying prayer, a kind of abridged confessional statement on which they could depend when needs arose. John the Baptist evidently taught his followers such a prayer. While Jesus intended His prayer for praying, it was also meant as a faith statement long before more detailed confessions became necessary.

A former parishioner of mine, Anne Hitchen of Long Beach, gifted at crocheting, made a 3' × 5' copy of the Lord's Prayer for me, which hangs in my study. When I look at that fascinating project, I don't marvel at the number of knots that comprise it, but how the Lord ties together in those few words such a magnificent summary of Christian concerns for God and oneself—in truth, for the whole family of faith, for it is a prayer prayed always in the plural. In chains of small knots, words grow together, and ideas become more than a string: a closely-tied summation of the graciousness of God. My mother has cross-stitched the Lord's Prayer in colorful threads that emphasizes the many hues hidden within these powerful words. Hanging above her bed, it reminds her of the rainbow of truths Jesus gave us in these brief words.

It is the abuse of these "knots" of meaning and "colors" of implication that offends the people of Varmland, to whom Selma Lagerlöf's Gösta Berling, a priest in the Church of Sweden, ministers, in her memorable novel. He is a drunken sot. The bishop has come to observe him conduct a service. The pastor stumbles in his drunkenness. He sees the parishioners as eager to rip his vestments from him and push him out into the street. Lagerlöf writes, "He had finished the Exordium, and he kneeled to say the Lord's Prayer." In the process he envisions his immediate dismissal from the ranks of the clergy, "a dishonored man for the sake of brandy." But, then, he vows to make his last time in the pulpit a chance to "testify to the glory of God." He puts his sermon notes aside and proclaims God's glory in such a way that the congregation, including the bishop, saw "the flame of inspiration burned in him" as he preached. Something happened to this man when he prayed the Lord's Prayer from a heart untainted by drink. To be sure, he was later to be dismissed; but for the moment the congregation and the bishop are mindful that God had put a call into Gösta Berling that they gladly recognize. Pastor Berling confessed a faith more than he prayed a prayer.[2]

Archbishop William Temple explains that "true prayer is always accompanied by appropriate conduct. Indeed, if prayer and conduct are both perfect, no distinction can be drawn between them. ... So the proper relation in thought between prayer and conduct is not that conduct is supremely important and prayer may help it, but that prayer is supremely important and conduct tests it."[3]

As we begin a venture through this gift of Jesus to all His disciples, let me share this interpretation with you:

The Lord's Prayer

An Informal Interpretation

> **Our:** In communion with Christ we are family with all who are His, linked together by divine grace, so that no human barriers divide us— neither race, nor ethnicity, nor language. Christ makes us one.

Father: There is intimacy in the family of the Savior. Jesus' Father is *our* Father, an ideal Father, who loves His children, chastising them when it is prudent, but more often than not providing them with encouragement to fully live as His redeemed children, with sanctified personalities that reflect Him and yet are distinctively personal. There is warmth in this relationship.

Who Art in Heaven: God's permanent home is in the celestial reaches of heaven, yet He makes His temporal home within the hearts of all His children as they dwell upon the earth He created.

Hallowed Be Thy Name: God's name speaks of His might and His graciousness in Christ as well as of His sinlessness and sanctity. We pray that our lives would honor and praise the holiness of His will.

Thy Kingdom Come: Our petition that the eternal kingdom may come soon recognizes that it comes to us daily in His Word. We pray, however (as Luther says of this petition[4]) "that God's name may be present through His holy Word *and our Christian lives*" (emphasis added).

Thy Will Be Done: We pray that the pure will of the loving God is fulfilled, including that we not be the accomplices of evil's will.

On Earth as It Is in Heaven: Heaven is heaven because God is present in all His glory, and evil is not. Only joy resides there. For that reason, we pray that earth may reflect its joy, even amid our trials and temptations, as we seek to live faithfully and lovingly for Him.

Give Us This Day Our Daily Bread: God is a compassionate Father, who seeks for His children to have food to eat, shelter from the night's cold, satisfying jobs, peace among nations, and all that is necessary to live healthy, useful lives. With thankful hearts, we beseech our Father for these daily needs, aware He has provided abundantly in the past, and we need but trust Him to guide us in making bread, in all its forms, available daily, today and tomorrow.

And Forgive Us Our Trespasses: Nothing we do can possibly earn forgiveness, but in Christ that forgiveness is assured. Thus we ask God to see us through the eyes of the Redeemer, who said of His tormentors, "Father, forgive them, for they know not what they are doing" (Luke 23:34).

As We Forgive Those Who Trespass against Us: Jesus wants us to know the fullness of forgiveness, and for that reason counsels us that we cannot hypocritically demand of God what we fail to share ourselves. Forgiveness is not just a high-sounding philosophy, but also a heartfelt desire of His people.

And Lead Us Not into Temptation: Life is not free of threats or pains, but God the Holy Spirit will see us through it all. Here we pray for faith and strength that will not fail us when we are plagued with troublesome ills.

But Deliver Us from Evil: When Satan's negative forces strike, we ask of the Lord that He will not let us slip into disbelief, but hang onto us until the ultimate victory that Christ assures is also ours.

For Thine Is the Kingdom: There are political boundaries and earthly rulers, but the kingdom that transcends all limitations is where our citizenship is now and eternally, and that kingdom is God's.

And the Power: We have no doubt about God's might and His ability to meet every need, whether we see that happening or not.

And the Glory Forever and Ever: We rejoice that the Triune God is present within the hearts of all believers even right now. He is extolled for the wonder of His love in the present time as well as in the time to come.

Amen: This is the seal of our vow, the assurance that our prayer is not idle talk, but sincerely prayed and confessed. "Yes," we affirm, "may every part of this prayer be swiftly and divinely answered. Yes, Lord, fulfill these words You have taught us. Yes, Lord, we believe You and You alone can answer our needs and do so with love."

This gift of Christ to His people is too marvelous to let become merely a rote recitation. It is, nevertheless, a prayer, The *Lord's* prayer. Pray it sincerely, but also confess it completely by living out its meaning in the world. Prayed by Christians around the world, it announces to the world the God in whom we trust and the faith we profess to believe. Writes Jan Milic Lochman, "Believers pray; those who pray believe."[5] In short, it is well that we pray both the Creed and the Lord's Prayer in addition to confessing them both in daily life. St. Paul advised Timothy in his Christian vocation to "fight the good fight of the faith. Take hold of the eternal life to which you were called when you made your good confession in the presence of many witnesses. In the sight of God, who gives life to everything, and of Christ Jesus, who while testifying before Pontius Pilate made the good confession, I charge you to keep this command without spot or blame until the appearing of our Lord Jesus Christ, which God will bring about in His own time—God, the blessed and only Ruler, the King of kings and Lord of lords" (1 Tim. 6:12–15).

Timothy's confession which Paul cites might include the one Jesus gave to the Twelve, "This, then, is how you should pray: Our Father in heaven ...."

OUR
FATHER

Our Father

Helmut Thielicke envisioned modern humanity as being somewhat like a person going through a forest in the pitch blackness of night.[1] He is all alone. There is no dialog. He does not know what specters lurk in the deepening shadows, nor is he aware if the disquieting noises are real threats or benign. He is filled with fear. If only he could speak with a guide who knows the forest well and could direct him to the other side! If only such a guide would ease his anxiety by assuring him of the guide's powerful ability to protect him! If only that guide could provide a pervasive light that would eliminate the shadows and push back the darkness! As the man considers these possibilities, he convinces himself that there is no such guide, there is only silence. He is persuaded that he is truly alone in the darkest forest one can imagine. He begins to talk to himself—out loud, nervously, awkwardly, but it works. He finds comfort in his own voice—momentarily—until he dissolves in fear and total fright, once more realizing there is no dialog. It is only a monolog. He has not changed, nor has the forest. No one has come. It is as fearsome as ever. He is as weak and as alone as before.

In life's forest God becomes more than a guide, but the forest's careful planter and knowing caretaker. The traveler, rather than talking with himself, receives genuine comfort while conversing with God. There is fellowship, community, dialog. The alien noises and threatening dangers are shrunk to human size, for God provides courage to battle the unknown unafraid. He sheds light where there was none before. He puts His arms around our shoulders, and we feel not only the personal touch but also His protective assurances. We hear more than our voice; we hear His.

Jesus demonstrated this magnificent dialog repeatedly to His disciples. He was one who prayed often. Up in the hills, out by the sea, in a quiet garden, Jesus prayed. He always returned to His colleagues more rested, more certain, more determined, more tranquil than before. No wonder they sought such a relationship themselves! In Jesus the Twelve saw more than a man in a forest, but one who stepped through the thickets of life briskly, unafraid, purposefully. If only He could teach them how it was done! That was the thought aching in heart and brain.

"Lord, teach us to pray ...," they begged (Luke 11:1). And Jesus did. "When you pray, say: Father ..." Then unfolded one of the most sublimely beautiful supplications ever to be spoken. Matthew makes the prayer's address even more meaningful. He quotes Jesus as beginning His prayer, "*Our* Father ...."

In this prayer that became for the followers of Jesus a creed, we discover that the key to marching through life's forest is not in going it alone but in eagerly confessing the marvelous relationship we have as trusting children of our caring Father. In addition to that, we discover our relationship to one another and the relationship to responsibility that comes from the intimate assurances of having such a Father. We are people wandering through a dark, frightening, world-encircling forest, who need a father who claims us, who gives us the faith we confess unitedly, whom we can trust.

While Luther, in both the Small and Large Catechisms, considers the first six words of the Lord's Prayer as an introduction, we will examine this marvelous salutation as not only an introduction, but primarily as a relationship, thus dividing the opening words into two parts: "Our Father" and (in the next chapter) "Who Art in Heaven."

The Emphatic "Our" and the Two-Way Relationship

The Lord's Prayer triggers an exciting confession. In two words we claim unity with one another as well as with God. This brief prayer of 69 words clearly reflects a two-way relationship. At the outset we pray, *"Our Father,"* words that have a family feel to them—meaning the family of believers.

I was surprised, then, during a local branch meeting of the National Conference of Christians and Jews. One Jewess asked that we conclude the meeting with the praying of the Lord's Prayer. She felt it was not singularly Christian, but a prayer anyone could pray. She praised its poetic beauty. Another applauded its universality. They spoke glowingly of its simplicity while honoring its startling profundity.

I understand the reason why non-Christians value this magnificent prayer as a universal expression. The word *our* seems to draw us into unity—if not in reality, then hoped for. However, the Lord's Prayer is exclusively the confessional prayer of Jesus of Nazareth. It was given by Jesus to His disciples to be *their* creedal prayer. It was to identify *them* as His followers. It is to be universal among His followers, not among those who disdain Him. To say "Our Father," then, implies that we can address God with the familiarity of the Son of God, who gave us the prayer. It is only through Jesus that this relationship becomes more than poetry, but fact; more than an ideal, but real. Its true value can be perceived only by those who pray it as disciples of the Teacher who gave it.

"An unbeliever," says Thomas Watson, "may call God his Creator, and his Judge, but not his Father. Faith legitimizes us, and makes us of the blood-royal of heaven ...."[2] As St. Paul taught the Galatians, "You are all children of God through faith in Christ Jesus" (3:26).

Christians may pray "Our Father" legitimately when they recognize not only their relationship to Him who is the God and Father of our Lord Jesus Christ, but when they also embrace all their fellow Christians in the oneness of discipleship. It does not mean they must approve heterodoxy, but that they recognize nevertheless something greater than differences. We confess here as in the Apostles' Creed "the holy Christian church, the communion of saints," an invisible unity that Christ Himself makes possible. By His Gospel, His messiahship, His sacrifice and Easter victory, we belong to each other.

Not every piece of a puzzle is the same shape or the same color, yet they fit together. So it is with the family of Christians. We are related to one another, because Jesus has made a relationship with His father possible via the cross. This is what we confess when we pray

"Our Father." We are pieces of a puzzle that comprise the Christian church—all of us together making up the picture that is Christianity. Just as the day of Pentecost found the apostles speaking in foreign tongues in the same setting of Jerusalem, so our varied means of expression of Christianity make us the church that adheres to the gospel of Jesus Christ. Even as 3000 Jews from around the globe were baptized in the name of Christ that day the Holy Spirit swept the church into being, so also that which makes us foreign to each other is overcome by that which makes us one: Jesus Christ. In two small words of no more than three syllables, we confess a relationship to God and to one another that Jesus makes happen: Our Father!

THE INTIMATE FATHER

The two-way relationship that unites the praying Christian with God is the tenderness of a paternal love that knows no rigid limits between divine parent and earthly child. God is not only our Father, He is far more intimately our *Daddy*. Whereas Matthew and Luke wrote their gospels in Greek, Jesus spoke Aramaic, a Semitic dialect prevalent then. As He addressed the heavenly Father in the Garden of Gethsemane by the familiar term *Abba* (Mark 14:36), so reason a number of New Testament scholars, Jesus first began the Lord's Prayer with that same intimacy: "Our Daddy." (St. Paul too learned to cry "Abba, Father," and so encourages us in Rom. 8:15–17 and Gal. 4:6–7).

"The address used by Jesus was *Abba*," writes Jan Milic Lochman. "This is a childlike and familiar diminutive. In Greek it would be *papa* rather than *pater*.... We are to understand *Abba* in the sense of covenant faithfulness and trust. In the witness of Jesus this relation binds the Father unconditionally to His children, come what may." It is not a sentimental use, a daring familiarity, a coarse and "sloppy fraternizing with God."[3] It is family intimacy.

One scholar illustrates this intimacy between God's children and the heavenly Father with a story about a triumphant Roman emperor. The emperor had the privilege of leading victorious armies through the streets of Rome in a great parade. There marched the conquering soldiers, their banners flying, their helmets gleaming, along with the ragtag defeated prisoners carrying the spoils of war. A small lad watched the great parade, cheering and shouting, until he saw the emperor's chariot. He jumped from the platform on which he sat, darted through the crowds, burrowed through the legions lining the route, and ran toward the emperor.

"You can't do that, boy," said a legionary, who swooped down and caught him, hoisting him into his muscular arms. "That's the emperor. You can't run down his chariot."

The tyke laughed and slithered down out of the soldier's grip, saying, "He may be your emperor, but he's my daddy."

"That," says Barclay, "is exactly the way the Christian feels towards God. The might, and the majesty, and the power are the might, and the majesty, and the power of one whom Jesus taught us to call *Our Father*" ... our Daddy.[4]

Jesus portrayed this enriching concept in the words of a parable. As He spoke about the prodigal son, He also unveiled the kindly, caring nature of the prodigal's father, who waits with open arms, ready to celebrate his son's return—a father who forgives (Luke 15:11–24). Nor is He an indifferent Father. "Which of you fathers, if your son asks for a fish, will give him a snake instead? Or if he asks for an egg, will give him a scorpion? If you then, though you are evil, know how to give good gifts to your children, how much more will your Father in heaven give the Holy Spirit to those who ask Him!" says Jesus (Luke 11:11–13).

"'Abba! Father!' These words are not a guarantee to us that there will be no sorrow," says Vernon Schreiber, "no questions, no times of terrible waiting, no cup of suffering, no cross in our lives. Nor will they automatically take us out of our own Garden of Gethsemane. But they will take us through Gethsemane and on to the cross, where we find in Christ the promise that there is one thing that He endured that you need never endure: the just retribution for our sin."[5]

Here is a relationship worth confessing often: God is truly a dear and loving Father.

ACCEPTING RESPONSIBILITY

In the two opening words of Jesus' most beloved prayer, we discover a sublime intimacy that makes our relationship exceedingly close and very dear. Then we learn something more. When we confess together "Our Father," we are also assuming another relationship: that of responsibility. We are responsible to God, but we are also responsible *for* and *to* one another.

A German theologian[6] has said rather forcefully that the Lord's Prayer "is not an egotistic religious prayer but a social kingdom prayer. It is not an *I* prayer but a *We* prayer. It is not a prayer for me but a prayer for us. If we come before God in true prayer, we do not simply come before the God who is our private God but before the God who is the God of us all."

The hinge by which this lid of the Lord's Prayer is opened is God's love through us. When we say "Our," it is as we love one another because Christ loves us. When we pray "Father," it is because His love so fills us that we must share it with all those around us, including those beyond the folds of Christianity. That's what sent Paul scurrying to Asia Minor and into Europe. It's what sent Peter on to Rome, Thomas to India, and others to Africa. It's that kind of love that changes pagan tribes into our brothers and sisters, and the unbelieving into members of God's family. It's that quality of love that drew an Indian chieftain, Noah Seattle, into the family of the faithful, and brought most of his tribes with him.

Just as we cannot pray "Our Father" and despise another Christian, so we cannot pray those words and disdain Muslim or Jew, Buddhist or Hindu. We are to love them eagerly as God's creations, although we reject their theologies intellectually and spiritually. To pray "Our Father" is to see Him as the ignored Father from whom they are estranged.

Likewise, we cannot pray "Our Father" and ignore the hungry and the homeless. They are members of His household. We cannot pray "Our Father" and neglect the starving children of Africa and the spiritually under-fed people of the former Eastern Bloc countries. We cannot pray "Our Father" and turn our heads from the sick and dying, from those addicted to drugs and those absorbed in themselves. We are responsible to God for their well-being, for their enlistment in the family of faith.

When we pray "Our Father," however, we are not praying alone—or fulfilling the needs of others all by ourselves. We are to do so collectively as the body of Christ, the church.

When we pray the Lord's Prayer, it is imperative we truly pray it—and *confess* it. It's then we are nurtured by it to act on our unity as God's people to minister to the needs of sheep not of this flock (John 10:16).

KEEPING VIGILANT

Do you sometimes feel like Helmut Thielicke's wanderer in life's forest, fearful and alone? Many an American Indian tribe practiced something called "The Vigil." As young boys grew, they were taught by their fathers how to survive in the rugged outdoors. As they grew older, they were readied to become braves in the tribe. Part of that training consisted of the boys being taken into the deepest, darkest part of the forest, where they were to spend the night—all alone. As dusk dimmed the light in the woods, the boy's father would turn and leave. The youngster was left alone. Surely, every hoot of the owl made him jump, every baying of a wolf at an unseen moon made him cringe, and every snap of twig by some wandering deer caused him alarm.

He had to spend the night alone, maintaining his courage in a frightful darkness, and waiting the long hours' passage in the agony of loneliness. Yet the Indian lad was not by himself. The father kept vigil with his son. He stationed himself secretly nearby, where he could keep watch over his child and be ready to protect him if danger came.

Sometimes we are unaware that God watches over us with more tenderness than that Indian father. All we need do is call upon Him, this eternal Father, this heavenly Daddy, as did Jesus: *Abba! Father!* He is nearer than the breeze that caresses you, no further than the left hand is from the right when it assumes the attitude of prayer.

WHO ART IN HEAVEN

WHO ART IN HEAVEN

A neighborhood letter carrier in my childhood days maintained that a lot could be told about people by their address. You didn't have to know them personally, the street address was enough. It may not be as easy now as then, but surely God's address tells us more than where His eternal home is.

Samuel Becket tells the story of Estragon and Vladimir in his tragicomedy *Waiting for Godot*. They don't know Godot or anything about him, yet they wait. They don't know how to get hold of him, let alone his address, yet they wait. They get messages from time to time saying Godot is coming soon, so they wait. When he doesn't show up, they want to leave, yet they cannot budge. They hang on because they realize that, once Godot comes, they will be "saved"—whoever Godot is.[1] Godot, if I caught the playwright's drift, is a pseudonym for God—the God who is, yet the God who, as with this unlikely pair, is all too frequently unknown.

Dr. Walter Maier, the late radio pulpiteer on "The Lutheran Hour," told a story about a well-decorated soldier who was attending a convention. As people streamed into the hall, the veteran walked up and down the aisles asking the spectators the plaintive question, "Can you tell me who I am?"

He was one of a million casualties of the war, the

tragic victim of amnesia, a man who, Dr. Maier said, "was mentally wounded and spiritually crushed by the brutality of bloodshed."[2] He didn't know who he was, let alone his home address. His dogtags had been lost, and no one knew the unit to which he belonged. Yet if he never discovered his earthly identity but trusted in the Jesus of the Lord's Prayer, he nevertheless had a heavenly one. For as heaven is God's address, so it has been given to everyone splashed by God's grace. As Paul writes, "Our citizenship is in heaven" (Phil. 3:20).

WHO GOD IS

"Our Father who art in heaven" reminds us who God is: the all-powerful, holy, and loving One. And, although we call Him Father, the phrase reminds us that He is most assuredly God, "maker of heaven and earth, of all that is, seen and unseen," as we say in the Nicene Creed.[3]

It is imperative that we recognize that this One we call *Abba* is not merely an improved and enlarged model of earthly dads, nor an aging sugar daddy who can be hornswoggled out of His kingdom. No, He is *God*—not with a small "g" as in "gods and goddesses," mind you, but *God* capitalized, with the article *the*, as in "*the* God who is God." Or, better yet, as St. Paul puts it, "The God and Father of our Lord Jesus Christ, the Father of compassion and the God of all comfort" (2 Cor. 1:3).

The Greek gods supposedly lived on Mount Olympus. Jupiter and Juno reigned from the temple atop Rome's Capitoline Hill. Baal and the Ashtoreths, among other high places, called Mount Carmel home. And

Egypt's god, Amon-Re, considered Karnak his sacred residence. When the Roman Caesar was deified, he was worshiped as a god who walked about openly. The heretical Samaritans worshiped God on Mount Gerezim, the observant Jews on Mount Zion; but the God and Father of our Lord Jesus Christ is not bound to earth, to cloud-covered mountains or marble-columned temples made with hands (2 Cor. 5:1). His home is heaven.

Heaven is not a geographic address, mind you; not even an astronomical one. Heaven is above us, as well as being within us. Did not the apostle John teach us, "No one has ever seen God; but if we love one another, God lives in us and His love is made complete in us" (1 John 4:12)? Heaven is "out there" while being "in here," in the heart. God's residence is remote only in the sense that we cannot control it or manage it or dominate it. If we could, God would not be God, nor would heaven be heaven. Despite its closeness within, it is not something we may own, but a home we may share—with its chief resident, the Triune God.

This address tells us a great deal about God, for it means that He is truly all-powerful. If He can be "out there" while being "in here," He is unlimited, boundless. He is no puppet for us to handle; no marionette whose strings we pull. He is fully God; not some idol of bronze or gold, plaster or marble. He lives, and He gives life. He sets the planets to spinning and the sun to shining (Ps. 8:3). He makes the winds blow and allows storms to swirl (Ps. 108:4; Is. 28:2).

We know that He is not only mighty, we know that He is holy; the Old Testament makes that distinctively clear. We know that He is loving; the New Testament underscores that in more than red print and luminescent yellow markings. In Jesus Christ, the Redeemer, the Victor over death, and the Master of life, we discover that God so loved us that He sent His only Son to rescue us. He abandoned His heavenly home so that "whoever believes in Him shall not perish but have eternal life," says John 3:16. That's what love does. It shares its address—at a costly price, out of genuine care. Thus we pray to the loving Father "who art in heaven."

THE GOD WHO IS AT HAND

He is not only the God with a heavenly address, but the God who is knowable—and approachable—by earthly believers. It is not a matter of waiting for Godot, but a matter of recognizing the Father by knowing the Son. We need not be perplexed by who and what the Father is like, for we have seen the Son—in miracles too many to number and messages too poignant to forget. "Like Father like Son," they say. Jesus phrased it more pointedly, "I and the Father are one" (John 10:30). Said Jesus to a perplexed Nicodemus who came to Him in the still secrecy of night, "I have spoken to you of earthly things and you do not believe; how then will you believe if I speak about heavenly things? No one has ever gone into heaven except the one who came from heaven, the Son of Man" (John 3:12–13). He spoke of Himself.

God is not wary of earth nor so bound up by the joys of His heaven that He is unapproachable. We need not wait for Him, for He has already found us. In gratitude we need only wait *upon* Him—through prayer, exercising it in faith in Christ and in hope through the

34

Holy Spirit, implementing our prayers in action, and nurturing them in His Word.

"Our Father who art in heaven" also reminds us that, as the Father, He heeds our needs. After giving the Our Father prayer to His hearers, Jesus encouraged them to pray by saying, "Ask and it will be given you; seek and you will find; knock and the door will be opened to you. For everyone who asks receives; he who seeks finds; and to him who knocks, the door will be opened. Which of you, if his son asks for bread, will give him a stone? Or if he asks for a fish, will give him a snake? If you, then, though you are evil, know how to give good gifts to your children, how much more will your Father in heaven give good gifts to those who ask Him!" preached Jesus (Matt. 7:7–11). The Father "who art in heaven" is approachable.

James tells us, "You do not have, because you do not ask God. When you ask, you do not receive, because you ask with wrong motives, that you may spend what you get on your pleasures" (James 4:2–3). God is reachable. We are to ask in the name and spirit of Christ. "If you remain in Me and My words remain in you, ask whatever you wish," says Jesus, "and it will be given you" (John 15:7). This not only requires the God of power, but the God who is reachable in Jesus Christ.

Martin Luther's barber, Peter Beskendorf, wanted a simple way to pray; so, as the disciples asked Jesus, this Wittenberger asked Luther how. The Reformer's response became a small tract entitled *A Simple Way to Pray, for a Good Friend.* Wrote Dr. Luther,

Dear Master Peter: I will tell you as best I can what I do personally when I pray. May our dear Lord grant you and to everybody to do it better than I! Amen.

Luther then wrote about diligence in praying, and added,

When your heart has been warmed by such recitation to yourself [of the Ten Commandments, the words of Christ, etc.] and is intent upon the matter, kneel or stand with your hands folded and your eyes toward heaven and speak or think as briefly as you can:

O Heavenly Father, dear God, I am a poor unworthy sinner. I do not deserve to raise my eyes or hands toward Thee or to pray. But because Thou has commanded us all to pray and hast promised to hear us and through Thy dear Son Jesus Christ has taught us both how and what to pray, I come to Thee in obedience to Thy word, trusting in Thy gracious promise. I pray in the name of my Lord Jesus Christ ... as He has taught us: Our Father who art, etc., through the whole prayer, word for word.[4]

Luther knew God to be reachable through His Son, despite His abode in heaven and the reformer's in Saxony. By that address Luther knew what God does. He loves us. Did not Isaiah quote God as saying, "As the heavens are higher than the earth, so are My ways higher than your ways and My thoughts than your thoughts" (Is. 55:9)? He is beyond our comprehending, but not beyond our spiritual reach—because He loves us.

WE BELONG TO GOD

The Father's address reminds us about even more: it reminds us whose we are. Although God is sinless and we are not, His love transcends the difference. Since we cannot reach heaven on our own, He brings it to us, bridging the distance of time and space, to make heaven *our* address as well as that of the Trinity. Thus, when we pray to our Father "who art in heaven," we are identifying His home as well as ours; for, you see, in this prayer we confess an allegiance that goes beyond the borders of our nation and the limits of this planet. We not only know who we are, but whose! Paul put it this way, "You are no longer foreigners and aliens, but you are fellow citizens with God's people and members of God's household, built on the foundation of the apostles and prophets, with Christ Jesus Himself as the chief cornerstone" (Eph. 2:19–20).

Mrs. Threadgoode knew that. You remember her— the elderly woman in the Rose Terrace Nursing Home in Fannie Flagg's novel *Fried Green Tomatoes at the Whistle Stop Cafe*. She knew heaven was her home. (I'm assuming that this fictional character was intended to be an actual Christian, one who trusted in Christ's salvation.) She told Evelyn Couch, her younger friend, "Sometimes I just cain't wait to get to heaven. I just cain't wait. The first thing I'm gonna do is look up old Railroad Bill. … Of course, he was colored, but I'm sure he'll be in heaven. Don't you think he'll be there, Evelyn?"[5] Mrs. Threadgoode may not have been an intellectual or as deeply religious as many, yet she knew whose she was (again, within my assumption). In a time and place when segregation saw a racially divided heaven, she saw God's children united in one eternal home. She knew God as a God within reach and heaven as a home for which to yearn.

There are many foreign gods that trap the souls and lives of people today. This pantheon includes the skittish god of pleasure and the greedy god of affluence, the lustful god of uncontrolled passions and the debilitating god of false security, the god of control and manipulation. But none of these deities resides in heaven. Their home is hell, and that's what they bring with them when they sweep into lives. Dazzled by their glittering glamour that masks their evil, we often fall prey to their clutches.

God, the Father of our Lord and Savior Jesus Christ, on the other hand, radiates the richness of heaven instead of the stench of hell. Claim the God of heaven, and you claim heaven as your home. You know whose you are.

St. Paul told the Philippians, "In everything, by prayer and petition, with thanksgiving, present your requests to God" (Phil. 4:6). Jesus said, "With God all things are possible" (Matt. 19:26). Another time, He told the father of an ailing boy, "Everything is possible for him who believes" (Mark 9:23). That doesn't sound like a God who is so exclusive that heaven never meets earth. He gives us the deed to eternity now by Christ's conquest of the cross.

Everett Fullam says that this is

the most central and sobering teaching of the Christian faith, that God at a real point in history came down ... and entered the world of our experience. In this boundless universe of galaxies, quasars and formations surpassing our wildest imaginations, this tiny little globe on which we live became in the words of J. B. Phillips, "the visited planet." God Himself, in the person of His Son, came among us.[6]

As a result, his address, heaven, is now our address too. We need not walk about with heads down and eyes closed. Since we are members of God's family and residents of heaven while still on earth, you and I can move forthrightly, knowing that God Himself goes with us.

The most dynamic people often are terminally ill Christians. They live as though they will never die. They work. They worship. They visit. They love. They trust the eternal Father, who brings heaven to them in Christ, so they can live triumphantly through days of pain and difficulty unafraid. They meet defeats, but they're not defeated. They encounter setbacks, but they move forward. Satan slaps them down, but God lifts them up— for they are citizens of His heaven, members of His family. They know whose they are.

If you, like Estragon and Vladimir, are waiting for God as they were waiting for Godot, wait no more; for our Father "who art in heaven" is here now, to be yours forever. In Christ we discover what He does. And in Jesus we find out whose we are, for that celestial address tells us this is one Father who does know best.

HALLOWED
BE THY NAME

HALLOWED
BE THY NAME

The engineered lines of a freeway are simple, but they are not simplistic. Hidden beneath the ribbons of concrete lie the details of engineering, of construction, of skill and labor. And, just as freeways require minute engineering detail, so does prayer. For instance, "Hallowed be Thy name," four gentle words, contain an amazing and awesome array of implications that we must pursue.

A friend of mine has watched every step of the construction of Highway 85's bridges that cross San Jose's Pearl Avenue and soar westward beyond Almaden Expressway. She has come to the conclusion that she never ever wants to drive across those bridges, for what she has seen has not convinced her that they are safe for fast-moving traffic or even slow-paced joggers. But she has not analyzed the engineering.

So it is with these four words. Until we examine them, we cannot know just how strong and sturdy they are in supporting us in our travel through life. "Hallowed be Thy name": that's our freeway now, the freeway of Christian life.

But what is important for our study? Malcolm Muggeridge remembers his youth and the headmaster at South Croydon Elementary School, who led the daily prayers. It was particularly important to "aspirate" (to enunciate distinctly) the "h" in "Hallowed be Thy name."[1] That may have been a teaching device useful for instructing children in proper enunciation, but the diction of the heart is needed more.

THE UNDERPINNINGS: GOD'S NAME

As we study this "road's" construction, we begin with the obvious. In this brief passage from the Lord's Prayer we speak of hallowing a name. It's a specific name. It's the name of God. We address Him as "Our Father" in this prayer, but that title is mostly a description of His relationship with us.

Some people don't have that relationship, much less know His name. Jimmy Dugan, the coach of the fictional Rockford Peaches in the movie *A League of Their Own*, attempts a prayer in the baseball team's locker room. A bit intoxicated and somewhat overwrought, he thanks God for a one-night stand with a South Bend waitress, and he squeezes out a hollow "hallowed be Thy name." Jimmy knew the phrase, but not the implications for life. Try as he did, he couldn't find the God whose name he sought to make holy. I suspect he didn't know Him by name at all.

The name of the Triune God which He revealed in the Old Testament is *Yahweh*, a genderless name. To the Jews that name was so holy that they dared not speak it; it could not even be whispered. As they read the Scriptures, they would use another name for God: *Adonai* in Hebrew, or *Kyrios* in Greek, meaning Lord. That, too, was a title rather than the intimate and personal name of

God. Human lips, they believed, were imperfect, therefore they must not utter the name of the one who is perfect. Instead, they employed a title, a reverent and honorable title.

Jesus invites us to hallow His name because to do so is to honor God Himself. For Middle Easterners, one's name is more than one's bond; it is the person himself. As one theologian explained, "The name of God stands for the whole being of God. To know His name is to know His character, His personality, His temperament, His love, His mercy, His power."[2]

Therefore, we hallow the *person* of God. That is, we sanctify God. Instead of making Him common, we revere Him as He is: holy, even without our hallowing of Him and His name. Yet, when we pray this petition, we also confess that we believe He is so holy that we shall not be among those who demean Him.

As we study the design of this highway of the Christian life, here is the structural steel: God's name. It spans the murky waters of uncertainty beneath and the quagmire of doubt nearby.

THE PAVING: SANCTIFYING HIS NAME

The second aspect of this freeway is the concrete paving. The four words "Hallowed be Thy name" are not merely an idle exclamation, they are a petition. We are *praying* that God's name be hallowed. The words are a plea that God be sanctified, not only by those who believe in Him but also by those who do not. This immense petition flows like a ribbon of ready-mix concrete from the Lord's Prayer onto the girders and framework of the Christian life.

This ribbon links every Christian with one another. It binds us to the world in which we live—for if this planet is abused, its riches squandered, its morality abandoned, and the whole place fouled to the point of hopelessness, the creator of this universe is not hallowed. Not at all. To hallow His name means to care for what is His.

Our confession of this creedal prayer is a renewing of our pact to be stewards of the earth. As we uphold the designer and builder of this universe, so we accept the role of steward, manager, in caring for it.

Curtis Mitchell points out that this petition, together with the remaining six, is stated as a command, not a plea. A literal rendering of the Greek would read, "Cause Your name to be hallowed."[3] In short, we are asking God for *His* active action in sanctifying His name in this world. We are pressing that He who has the authority and the power remind us that God truly is God.

Sweden's King Charles XII, who battled Peter the Great across much of Eastern Europe, was not a popular man in his homeland. The Swedes had lost vast colonies and countless lives as well as great riches because of the aspirations of their monarch. Yet he was a daring man. One time, the king decided to visit Karlstad, a city in the middle of the kingdom, without fanfare. He rode alone and arrived on a Sunday as the people were in church. Disheveled and dirty from his exhausting ride, he nevertheless entered the packed church to worship. There were no seats left, so he just leaned against a wall unnoticed to hear the sermon already in progress. An old man, perhaps a soldier who had served under Charles XII, recognized him immediately. The old man stood erect and respectful. Others, hearing it whispered, arose also, so that before long the whole church was standing in honor of their king. Although these people had cursed the king many times for their enormous losses in human life and national wealth, when they saw him, "they were immediately under his dominion."[4]

Some Christians act as if they have never seen their king. Their faith is so weak that one wonders how often they ignore Him in their daily walk. But when He appears on the Last Day and forgives their weakness, will they not also stand tall and honor Him then? If so, their gelatinous spiritual spines will become as steel and concrete.

Signs along the Way: Praising God's Name

If God's name is the structural steel of this phrase in Jesus' prayer, and if its petitionary nature is the concrete that paves this freeway, then praise can be understood as the lane stripes, the directional signs, the lights, and the landscape. Whatever else Jesus intended this prayer to be and do for the Twelve, it was certainly proposed to be a means to give God glory.

Long before the towers and steeples of Gothic cathedrals scratched the sky and jewel-toned windows filled their buttressed walls with sparkling light, humankind was hallowing God. In simple songs and complex cantatas, in the thunderous sounds of organ pipes and the haunting sound of woodwinds, in the rich harmony of strings and the blare of brass, in solo voice and massive choirs, people have hallowed God with music, glorying in His love. In pen and ink, in oil and watercolor, in magnificent murals, spectacular mosaics, and tiny illuminated letters on handwritten books, artists have added their praise of the God who humbles man with the gentle beauty of a wild flower as well as the greater gift of the Gospel. In marble and ironwood, in oratory poetry, God has been proclaimed and God has been hallowed. Yes, life itself glorifies God. "Hallowed be Thy name," we pray—not so that monuments may be built, but that lives may radiate a sanctity that honors the Triune God in word and deed.

The highway of life is well-marked when it has the signs of praise in ready evidence, when despite the ills of life, people see the greater gift of God's healing and sing to His honor. Instead of reeling in the plague of sin, they revel in the joy of Jesus.

How is the freeway of your life marked? With the signs of praise and the striping of adoration? Is it lighted with the bright globes of Christian love? That's what it means to not only pray "Hallowed be Thy name," but to act it out in life.

Consider the life of Raoul Wallenberg, this nation's second honorary American. Educated here, he was the heroic Swedish diplomat whom President Roosevelt and King Gustav V sent to Hungary to rescue the remaining Jews in the last days of World War II. Among those rescued were Congressman Tom Lantos and his wife.

In 1984, while I was standing on Wallenberg Street

in Budapest, a woman came up to me and said in a heavy accent, "You Svedish?"

"No. American."

"Wallenberg," she said, pointing to the memorial marker on the corner of an apartment house there. "Wallenberg a good man. He helped me." I was astonished to meet one of those who had survived the Holocaust. Wallenberg had hallowed God's name in such a way that many still remember what this Christian did for Jews. He left his mark of praise of God upon everyone he rescued. He let light shine in the darkness. He marked the way for others to freedom.

Are the signs of your praise lining your freeway of life? You may not be able to rescue 120,000 people, but maybe you can help one homeless person or one family without work. Hallow God's name by befriending your fellow human beings through emergency relief efforts, local pantries, family shelters, foreign missions, local homes for the aging, world hunger ingatherings, and countless similar assistance means. Illuminate the spiritual freeway with the light of love. By loving God, you love others. By loving others, you hallow His name. Action is the sign of your freeway's direction.

THE COMPLETED SPAN

It is a massive structure, this freeway of the Christian life. It is undergirded with the sturdy steel of God Himself. It is paved with the smooth concrete of petitions that glorify God. It is lined, marked, lighted, and landscaped with our actions of praise.

Forty years ago I drove on my first freeway. I didn't

want to. I had just come from the quiet hills of the Midwest and was relatively inexperienced in metropolitan traffic, let alone a Los Angeles freeway. But my hostess was bound and determined that I learn how. Initially, other cars wouldn't let me on the freeway; and once I got there, they seemed determined to make me leave. Its dangers and delays were frightening at the outset, but now I regard a freeway as the only way to travel.

When we pray and confess "Hallowed be Thy name," we are swinging onto the freeway of life. When we honor God as both the creator of life as well as the engineer of salvation, we need never fear that the steel supports will weaken or the concrete paving will crack or that we'll get lost in the blur of unregulated spiritual traffic as we confess the Lord's Prayer by a life that goes full speed down the freeway to joy.

THY KINGDOM COME

THY KINGDOM COME

Whoopi Goldberg portrays a Reno mobster's girl-friend in the film "Sister Act." She witnesses a killing and reports it to the authorities, who send her to a San Francisco nunnery for protection from a "contract" that the mob is anxious to fulfill. She's a cabaret singer, a gangster's girl, a woman who knows the flamboyant life of gambling and loose living. Being in a convent isn't exactly her cup of tea.

"What am I going to do here," she asks, "pray?"

"Pray!" answers her police protector wisely.

To a goodly number of people in this world, prayer *is* outmoded. With computers and FAX machines, cellular phones and electronic notebooks, CD-ROMs and VCRs, prayer seems a little tame. With dazzling neon lights, sequin-covered dresses and dancing, drinking, and gaming until all hours, prayer to Whoopi's character appears more than a little antiquated; it is passé.

Although Whoopi Goldberg feels like a fish out of water in that convent, she makes an attempt to pray. She mixes phrases of the Lord's Prayer with words of the Pledge of Allegiance as she says grace. If (as I suspect) Whoopi's character was touched by the Holy Spirit, who reawakened faith in her while in the convent, then it wasn't long before she caught certain rhythms and found a way to make music out of prayer and turn apathy into praise.

Bandini, the aspiring writer in John Fante's novel *Ask the Dust*, has had his education in a parochial school and the streets of a largely immigrant community. He has done some reading, however, and has been persuaded that Christianity has its limitations. Yet a poignancy pulls within his heart as he prays, "Almighty God, I am sorry I am now an atheist, but have You read Nietzsche? Ah, such a book! Almighty God, I will play fair in this. I will make You a proposition. Make a great writer out of me, and I will return to the church. And please, dear God, one more favor: make my mother happy. I don't care about the old man; he's got his wine and his health, but my mother worries so. Amen."[1]

Whoopi's character and Bandini both have limited views of God and the magnificent gift of prayer, but both—though they try to deny or ignore Him—realize God cannot be overlooked. Nor can they bypass the reality of His kingdom.

Nor can we. Therefore, we pray as Jesus taught us, "Thy kingdom come," confessing it with the depth of true sincerity, aware that the kingdom requires an explanation, an exploration, and exploitation.

AN EXPLANATION

At the time of Jesus, all lands were kingdoms. There were empires with emperors, monarchies with monarchs, principalities with princes, and nomadic tribes with Bedouin chieftains. There were moguls and potentates, autocrats, tyrants, dictators, and despots. Whether bounded by borders or not, the world was comprised of territorial kingdoms.

Jesus dwelled in the tetrarchy of Herod Antipas, the princely son of a kingly father, Herod the Great. The Lord visited Jerusalem, the center of Jewish faith and the capital of a tiny kingdom of Jews. Both the Galilean tetrarchy and the Jewish kingdom were realms of the Empire of Rome, the mighty domain of Caesar. Emperors were kings of kings. But Jesus did not ask us to pray for a kingdom of real estate with knights and castles, jeweled crowns and ermine-lined cloaks. It is God's kingdom for which we pray "Come!"

The second-century church father Irenaeus writes that the kingdom of God involves the renewal of creation. Seventeenth-century theologian Thomas Watson wrote 96 pages on the Second Petition alone, saying God's kingdom is a kingdom of grace and glory. Everett Fullam says it's a real kingdom, "a sphere of sovereignty, of rule, and it has a king." Walter Rauschenbusch says it is a "precious truth," and from that he produced the social gospel. Dietrich Bonhoeffer suggests the kingdom is a kind of wandering. Herbert Girgensohn says the kingdom is an "event," and beyond that it is "the world of life." Karl Hertz has emphasized that "the kingdom of God must be conceived in terms of the Gospel, not the Law." Kurt Rommel holds that "God's kingdom is His power." William Barclay asserts it is His will. John Bright holds that the kingdom of God "is the unifying note of the biblical Word ... [and] still the motivating force of the living church." Martin Luther says the kingdom of God is the fulfillment of the Apostles' Creed and is a kingdom of grace. Helmut Thielicke teaches us "that the kingdom of God is not a state or condition of this world, not an ideal order of nations and life ..., but that it centers about a *person:* The king, God Himself ..." Thielicke goes on to say elsewhere, "The kingdom of God is where Jesus is ...."[2]

To these explanations, C. S. Lewis adds others which he calls "festoons." He understands the term *kingdom* on three differing levels:

> First, as in the sinless world beyond the horrors of animal and human life; in the behavior of stars and trees and water, in sunrise and wind. May there be *here* (in my heart) the beginning of a like beauty. Secondly, as in the best human lives I have known: in all the people who really bear the burdens and ring true, and in the quiet, busy, ordered life of really good families and really good religious houses. May that too be 'here.' Finally, ... in the usual sense: as in Heaven, as among the blessed dead.[3]

What is the kingdom which we pray to come? It is more than land and titles, more than property and privileges, but something wondrously magnificent.

John the Baptist came preaching the "Gospel of the kingdom." He called for repentance and said, "The kingdom of heaven is near" (Matt. 3:2). Jesus expanded on that theme, but His expansion was more than verbal; it included action. He healed the sick and quieted troubled hearts with forgiveness. He brought peace and wholeness and joy to the lives of the troubled. Before He healed the paralyzed man, He said, "Take heart, son; your sins are forgiven." Then He told him, "Get up, take your mat and go home" (Matt. 9:2–8). Here were the evidences of the coming kingdom that Malachi the prophet had foretold: "You who revere My name, the sun of righteousness will rise with healing in its wings" (4:2).

Jesus, of course, also proclaimed the kingdom in words. He told Pontius Pilate, "My kingdom is not of this world" (John 18:36). He said to Nicodemus, "No one can see the kingdom of God without being born from above" (John 3:3 NRSV). He sent others out to tell the surrounding communities, "The kingdom of God is near" (Luke 10:1–12). Jesus said of the scribe who understood that the great commandment is to love God and others as oneself, "You are not far from the kingdom of God" (Mark 12:28–34). He told the Pharisees who asked when the kingdom of God is coming, "The kingdom of God does not come with your careful observation, nor will people say, 'Here it is,' or 'There it is,' because the kingdom of God is within you" (Luke 17:20–21).

Having the kingdom within is another description of having Jesus Himself live in you. It underscores His love. It makes clear His forgiveness. It means eternal peace. It radiates joy. Out of the pages of Scripture, the words of Christ, and the interpretation of the learned, we discover that the explanation of this remarkable kingdom is wrapped up in the lived-out Gospel. That's why it is near and yet something to continue to pray that will come this day and the next and on into eternity itself. But if you need a one-word explanation, just say "Jesus." The kingdom of God is summed up in Him, the Prince of Peace and King without peer.

Explained Paul, "The kingdom of God is not a matter of eating and drinking, but of righteousness, peace and joy in the Holy Spirit" (Rom. 14:17). Now that's a kingly explanation—and it still means Jesus is Lord, the king of the everlasting kingdom.

Launching an Exploration

Since the kingdom of God is the theme of the whole Bible, Old and New Testaments, as John Bright teaches, and since it is centered in Jesus Christ and His Gospel, this kingdom has dimensions, dimensions we may explore. They are past, present, and future. They have height and depth.

Jesus taught that the ancient patriarchs, Abraham, Isaac, and Jacob, are in the kingdom of God (Luke 13:28), a fact that looks to the past. Jesus also assured us that the kingdom has a present reality: "The kingdom of God is within you" (Luke 17:21). And in His magnificent confessional prayer, Jesus taught all His followers throughout time to look to the future and pray "Thy kingdom come." Says the Lord in John's Revelation, "I am the Alpha and the Omega, ... who is, and who was, and who is to come, the Almighty" (1:8). In those words and these truths is the three-dimensional depth of this kingdom for which we pray.

Paul saw those dimensions as an infinitude: "I am convinced that neither death nor life, neither angels nor demons, neither the present nor the future, nor any powers, neither height nor depth, nor anything else in all creation, will be able to separate us from the love of God that is in Christ Jesus our Lord" (Rom. 8:38–39). Once again, it is Jesus Himself who personifies this wondrous kingdom.

The difficulty is that, in Jesus' day as well as long before and for generations afterward, some Jews looked upon this petition as something external. The rabbis, we're told, had long taught that these words should be the important ingredient of *all* prayers.[4] These words in the Lord's Prayer were not necessarily original with Jesus, you see, although His meaning was thoroughly new. The Jews who prayed these words, however, took them to mean an end to Roman rule and the establishment of an autonomous political kingdom of their own, and no more.

Even today, some people look upon the establishment of the State of Israel in 1948 as a partial fulfillment of this age-old rabbinic petition. But such a one-dimensional view limits this petition from the broad width Jesus intends. The kingdom He proclaimed is to extend from eternity to eternity and from its unfathomable depth to its incalculable height—its mystery and mystical meanings. If limited to political frontiers and government, the kingdom is no longer either the kingdom of God or the kingdom of heaven. The kingdom of God is much bigger and needs a much larger messiah than the Israeli Prime Minister. This three-dimensional kingdom—past, present, and future—has such a Messiah, one who fits its immense dimensions: Jesus!

As Jesus sent the Seventy out to witness for the kingdom, He instructed them to say, "Peace to this house." Jesus explained, "If a man of peace is there, your peace will rest on him; if not, it will return to you" (Luke 10:1–12). This is not a peace signed in surrender or as a treaty, but a peace that is given to those who will receive it. Jesus had the Seventy use the blessing of peace as a means of exploration of the kingdom. Jesus sent the Seventy out to share peace and by so doing to share the kingdom.

We receive that peace as a gift of grace. We are residents of the kingdom of God, for the Holy Spirit has bestowed upon us citizenship in a kingdom that has no end. He invades our lives to guide us. He gives us the Gospel, and Christ becomes our king in a kingdom without borders, a kingdom without limits, a kingdom that it takes a lifetime to explore. Jesus Christ revealed to John this promise: "Be faithful, even to the point of death, and I will give you the crown of life" (Rev. 2:10).

Explore the citizenship God has given you. Discover the peace it provides, the love that undergirds it, the forgiveness God grants daily to the repentant, the joy it manifests. Explore that citizenship, and you will find yourself within this kingdom without boundaries and this monarchy without taxes—and you will discover it is within you. And that brings joy!

Spiritual Exploitation

Since the kingdom of God is all that the Bible teaches, then you and I must not limit ourselves by exercising its message in half-hearted ways; we need to exploit it. We need to live as fellow members of the kingdom, as those whom God uses to hasten its coming. There is excitement in being a part of this kingdom, and the joy is in sharing it.

Curtis Mitchell reminds us that the petitions are all stated as commands.[5] This Second Petition is a demand that God once again bring His kingdom into our lives, now, as well as into the lives of everyone. It is a plaintive command that God not delay in coming again. It echoes the apostle John, who responded to the Lord's promise of "I am coming soon" by praying "Come, Lord Jesus" (Rev. 22:20).

How may we exploit this petition to its fullest for the world's benefit? Is it not by going out as the Seventy did? If we bring Christ to another house, we bring more than peace; we bring the kingdom. If we share the Gospel with yet another family, we enlarge our own—and recognize that the kingdom's limits are big enough for all. Our going forth, however, dare not be a sour sharing of this message, even if some Christians live life as if eating unripened persimmons. Love is not dyspeptic, but buoyant with the love of Christ and forgiving with the stain of His blood and the bright sunshine of His rising etched upon it. The kingdom may come through you to those you don't even know—if you let the gospel of Christ be demonstrated in your words, your actions, your attitudes, your lives.

During His last week of earthly ministry, Jesus sweat great drops of blood, and He bled again as nails pierced His flesh. Yet we do not hear Him accuse His enemies and vilify them. He brought the kingdom to the cross: "Father, forgive them, for they do not know what they are doing," He said of His executioners (Luke 23:34). His own team had failed to stand up for the kingdom in those last days. Judas betrayed Him. Peter denied Him. Yet Jesus did not cave in.

What was the cause, the goal, the purpose for which He struggled, asks Carl Braaten. "It was the *righteousness* of God's kingdom, that it might come to sinners, to make them clean. It was the *riches* of the kingdom, that it might come to poor people, to fill them with good things. It was the *freedom* of the kingdom, that it might come to people in bondage. It was the *light* of the kingdom, that it might come to blind people. It was the *health* of the kingdom, that it might come to lame, sick, and crippled people. That was the cause; it was a good cause" (emphasis added).[6] Jesus weathered doubt and suffering, pain and sacrifice, but He did not abandon the kingdom; He insured it. He exploited it for us, so that we might exploit its gifts for others.

The kingdom is ours because He gives it to us. He makes us members of it, not peasants and peons but members of the blood royal, princes and princesses, who not only know how to pray "Thy kingdom come," but how to share its invitation.

This is the kingdom we need to exploit—to the benefit of the world and the glory of God, as well as for the joy it grants.

Surely if Whoopi Goldberg's character could catch that reality, there should be no doubt in our mind that Christian prayer is worthy of concentration, and that God's kingdom is well worth the continuing petition, "Thy kingdom come!"

THY WILL BE DONE ON EARTH AS IT IS IN HEAVEN

THY WILL BE DONE
ON EARTH AS IT IS IN HEAVEN

Have you ever picked up a seed and wondered how the Creator could package so much tree in one tiny seed? Or how He could possibly store up such massive power in one infinitesimal atom? God has the marvelous ability to put little drops of water together to form massive oceans, to pile dust particles upon dust particles until they create a continent, and to accumulate so many tiny snowflakes that they make great glaciers.

We see a similar trait in God's Son. Jesus is able to say volumes in a few simple words. Take "Thy will be done on earth as it is in heaven," for instance. Here is compressed a total encyclopedia of ideas, a whole library of theology in a handful of simple words. In 11 words, Jesus teaches us to pray that God's heaven would embrace the earth, that His outlook encompass ours so that we see life and living as He does. In a little less than a dozen words, the Lord speaks of both the awesome wonder of God's will as well as humanity's free will. But Jesus had no intention of inserting a lengthy lecture into the middle of His brief prayer. Instead, He compacted it into a seed. He gave us an atom of sacred thought to energize our minds and empower our souls. Jesus taught His disciples to pray "Thy will be done on earth as it is in heaven" and, thereby, to let the implications grow in their hearts.

Admittedly, it is impossible to define this petition completely. Yet it is essential that we know something about God's will and the earth's need for it.

Billy Graham says, "The most important thing in life is doing the will of God." Dante Alighieri wrote in *The Divine Comedy*, "In His will is our peace." Herbert Girgensohn says, "God *is* will, the strongest of all wills, a will that prevails in every circumstance against every will that opposes it. It is a moral, holy will which does not allow itself to be mocked." A striking quotation concludes Malcolm Muggeridge's prayer in his *Confessions of a Twentieth-Century Pilgrim*. (Muggeridge was known earlier in life as a "vociferous unbeliever.") His words: "Help me to serve only Thy purposes, to speak and write only Thy words, to think only Thy thoughts, to have no other prayer than: 'Thy will be done.'" C. S. Lewis, in a personal letter, underscored that God's will be done: "The petition is not merely that I may patiently suffer God's will but also that I may vigorously do it. It must be as an agent as well as a patient. I am asking that I may be enabled to do it. In the long run I am asking to be given 'the same mind which was also in Christ.'"[1]

What is this will of God, and how may it be accomplished on earth? How can it fit into our secularized society? These are the questions that plague us. Though we may just barely scratch the surface, read on.

GOD'S HOLY WILL

Gideon, the fifth Old Testament judge, was uncertain about God's will. Though the angel of the Lord had appeared to him and had instructed him to lead Israel against the Midianites, the message did not seem correct to Gideon. He was no warrior, no general awaiting an army to lead into victorious battle. "How can I save Israel? My clan is the weakest in Manasseh, and I am the least in my family," argued Gideon (Judges 6:15).

The Lord assured him, "I will be with you, and you will strike down all the Midianites together" (6:16).

That was hard for Gideon to accept. He wasn't sure it was God who was speaking, much less that the message was true. Thus he tested God. He put a wool fleece on the threshing floor, saying, "If there is dew only on the fleece and all the ground is dry, then I will know that You will save Israel by my hand, as You said" (6:37).

The next morning, Gideon squeezed a bowl full of water from the drenched fleece. Yet Gideon was still uncertain, so he asked God to reverse the sign, to drench the ground around the fleece the next night, while keeping the sheepskin dry. Once again God fulfilled the assurances Gideon demanded, and he knew the will of the Lord.

But what about us? We have no assurance that God will speak directly with us as He did Gideon, nor has He told us to expect such messages—or such proof.

None of us can know fully the *mind* of God, but we can know something of His *will*. We know at least that His will is perfected in heaven, where in utter joy the angels respond to it (Rev. 5:11–12). But, how can we on earth know the will of God?

We can go to the one place where we know God shows us His will, Scripture, and to the Son of God who is revealed there. He explained, "I have come down from heaven not to do My will but to do the will of Him who sent Me" (John 6:38). Another time, He told the disciples, "My food ... is to do the will of Him who sent Me and to finish His work" (John 4:34). His work, His will, is our salvation. Did not John remind us, "For God so loved the world that He gave His one and only Son, that whoever believes in Him shall not perish but have eternal life" (John 3:16)? Paul says it a little differently, "[Jesus] gave Himself for our sins to rescue us from the present evil age, according to the will of our God and Father" (Gal. 1:4).

But the foundation for our salvation through Christ is God's constant love (John 3:16), a love that we saved ones are to live out in our own lives. That too is God's will. "'Teacher, which is the greatest commandment in the Law?' Jesus replied: ' "Love the Lord your God with all your heart and with all your soul and with all your mind." This is the first and greatest commandment. And the second is like it: "Love your neighbor as yourself." All the Law and the Prophets hang on these two commandments' " (Matt. 22:36–40). "My command is this: Love each other as I have loved you" (John 15:12). "For whoever does the will of My Father in heaven is My brother and sister and mother" (Matt. 12:50). However, "Not everyone who says to me, 'Lord, Lord,' will enter the kingdom of heaven, but only he who does the will of My Father who is in heaven" (Matt. 7:21).

Thus, when we pray "Thy will be done on earth as it is in heaven," we are confessing that we have received salvation in Christ, the benefit of God's will of love, and we are praying that God's Spirit so live in us that His will of love becomes our will—in faith and in action. It is

His will that we pray for the perfect will of the Father to be exercised among us in an imperfect world.

Putting God's will of love into action may cause us to suffer, as Peter points out in his first letter (1 Peter 3:17). God's will of love is not simple morality or mere pious living. It has a sanctified center: God's love. Therefore, Peter's emphasis is not on suffering but enduring, because love turns purposeless pain into purposeful gain. Jesus demonstrated that by His own life and sacrifice on the cross. Is that not heaven brought to earth, God's will made known in the realm of humanity?

No wonder, then, He taught us to pray "Thy will be done on earth as it is in heaven." It is so that we may be with Him.

God's Will and Our Earth

To say that God's will is that we love one another is to make a broad statement. What God calls us to do is to apply it to particulars.

Some people, however, fear the will of God, because they have assigned to His ultimate will some of the most diabolical events that darken history. If a child dies of some malevolent disease or a drive-by shooting, or a mother is killed by a drunk driver, someone will try to comfort the family by saying, "It was God's will." If tragedy strikes—the earth shakes violently and thousands are made homeless, or a tornadic cloud turns a residential neighborhood into kindling wood, or a great tsunami crushes a landscape for hundreds of miles inland, killing everyone in its path—some will say, "It's God's will."

God, of course, has used what looks like tragedy to accomplish His good will. Consider the destruction of Jerusalem and the Babylonian captivity. Yet, heaven is not fraught with devilish ills. It's Satan who foists his evil upon us in criminal fashion. And, evil will continue to exist in this fallen world in spite of our prayers. So, when it slams us broadside, we can but turn to the Lord, knowing that, in spite of evil, God is good and He has His blessings lined up for us. At those times, we pray "Thy will be done," not even knowing what His will is other than our salvation.

God's ultimate will, of course, is the salvation of all humanity. But He also wills that we live in peace and harmony with one another. "Stop doing wrong, learn to do right! Seek justice, encourage the oppressed. Defend the cause of the fatherless, plead the case of the widow" (Is. 1:16b–17). And the Law condemns us when we don't. But such admonitions are not given merely to the generic "everyone"; they are laid upon Christians especially (see the epistle of James). True, such earthly peace will not grant eternal salvation to anyone, but it still stands as one of God's intermediate purposes. And one way His heavenly will is brought to our earth is by living out this petition ourselves.

That certainly implies that we don't need to let drug lords take over seemingly helpless neighborhoods, or allow alcohol's use to crush families, or permit economic distress to sweep whole generations into the dustbins. Indifference is the devil's mode. Apathy is Satan's tool. Permitting evil to swamp the innocent and injustice to infect whole elements of our society is to fail to act on the prayer we so often and so glibly pray: "Thy will be done on earth as it is in heaven." We need the courage to act on our prayers.

Archbishop Nathan Söderblom of the Church of Sweden says, "A place of honour is due to those saints of religion who have put their whole soul into serving and apprehending God's will in *history*." A human being can see nothing "so long as he is standing as a mere spectator; only those who serve God fully and self-sacrificingly can perceive God's will."[2] In short, we must act on our prayers, confessing them by the lives we live and the deeds we do.

One of Scripture's images of heaven is that of no more hunger (Rev. 7:16). Surely we can bring a taste of heaven to earth—God's will matched with man's need—by feeding the hungry. When you help stock community pantries, when you give funds for family shelters, you are letting God's arms wrap around the needy, and heaven's will is being done. You are making the Third Petition an active verb—with the personal pronouns "I" and "me" part of it.

GOD'S WILL AND OUR NATION

There is one more point that I wish to make. Despite a variety of Supreme Court decisions and innumerable political documents that seem to deny this nation's Christian past, we need to insist on God's will for daily life in America. That's needed as much now as in the days when Jesus first gave the prayer to the Twelve.

Our historic separation of church and state is not as "clean" as some would have us believe. Today's passion for a separation that virtually denies religion has reached an understanding our forefathers never had in mind. Nine of the original 13 colonies had their own established churches before the Revolution. From New York southward to Georgia, the colonies each had a state religion. The last colony to finally separate itself from a state church was Massachusetts—in 1833, 58 years after the Declaration of Independence.[3]

Religion was important to the founding fathers. Out of 916 political writings written by prominent Americans between 1760 and 1805, 3,154 religious quotations were identified, 34% of them from the Bible.[4]

Of our religious foundation, W. B. J. Martin tells us,

> The Fourth of July was a venture of faith, not a mere gesture of rebellion. And it raised as its standard, not a flag but a document ... The Declaration of Independence. That document, of course, is rooted in the Scriptures. Not only are its phrases lifted from the Bible in general terms, but they are definitely linked with the experience of the chosen people. They echo and reflect the Passover syndrome: slavery in Egypt, and the flight into the wilderness, the great trek to the promised land, and over all, the guiding hand of God.[5]

In fact, the words of The Declaration of Independence echo the sermons of a Congregationalist pastor, the Rev. Jonathan Mayhew, who preached exactly the same ideas some 26 years before.[6]

Under the new Constitution of the United States, Vice President John Adams is reported to have said, "We have no government armed with power capable of contending with human passions unbridled by morality and religion. Our constitution was made only for a moral and a religious people. It is wholly inadequate for the government of any other."

I cite these examples to say that, 200 years ago, Christians faithfully acted upon this petition, "Thy will be done on earth as it is in heaven." They influenced, in a positive way, the establishment of this nation. They did not perceive a secularized life that had no Christian influence. We wrong our nation—and disavow the Third Petition—when we fail to be involved in the political system today. This prayer impels us to vote and to do so intelligently. It demands our involvement with local government and organizations so that Christian ideologies are invested in American life—so that heaven meets earth, and God's will affects God's people and this nation with love and true happiness, the pursuit of which is one of our freedoms.

We have no need for a state religion, but we have every need for religious people to state emphatically affirmations of the Christian faith in American life that insure wholesome living and human morality. God accomplishes His will on earth through His people. We bring that will to this nation when we live its message, not behind closed doors but in the public marketplace as well as the statehouse, in the nation's capitol, and in every town hall from Maine's rock-bound coast to California's white-sand beaches.

After his visit to the riot-torn regions of Los Angeles following the Rodney King verdict, Patrick Buchanan tried to analyze the reasons for the rampage.

Where did the mob come from? Well, it came out of public schools from which God and the Ten Commandments and the Bible were long ago expelled. It came out of corner drug stores where pornography is everywhere on the magazine rack. It came out of movie theaters and away from TV sets where macho violence is romanticized. It came out of rock concerts where rap music celebrates raw lust and cop-killing. It came out of churches that long ago gave themselves up to social action, and it came out of families that never existed. If they didn't know any better, perhaps they were never taught any better. ... For decades, secularists have preached a New Age gospel, with its governing axiom: There are no absolute values in the universe; there are no fixed and objective standards of right and wrong. There is no God. It all begins here and it ends here. Every man lives by his own moral code. Do your own thing. And the mob took them at their word, and did its own thing."[7]

This nation needs a populace of Christians who do not hide their faith nor permit unwholesome laws, life, and immoral liberty to stain the history that began with Christian witness and hope. When we *in* America pray "Thy will be done on earth as it is in heaven," we are also praying *for* America (as well as for all nations), that "they may see your [our] good deeds and glorify God on the day He visits us" (1 Peter 2:12).

Being Willing, Not Willful

Packed into this small package of words in the Lord's Prayer is a mighty confession. We believe God's will needs to form man's will. We believe God's people are the instruments by which that will is promulgated among us. And we believe that heaven chases hell, as each Christian exemplifies God's will in a living confession of it.

The Rev. Peter Gabriel Muhlenberg served a Lutheran parish in Virginia's Shenandoah Valley. One Sunday morning in 1776, vested for worship, he preached and conducted the service. At the end of the liturgy, he entered the sacristy, removed his robes, and marched into the church wearing the uniform of a colonel in Virginia's revolutionary army. He shocked not only his congregation, but everyone in Virginia.

"Roll the drums for recruits!" he instructed, and a drummer boy broke the solemn silence of the Sabbath with a tattoo that called every able-bodied man from the congregation to live out his faith and to do so within the Eighth Virginia Regiment. Before nightfall, 300 men had joined him.[8]

God calls you too to a revolution: to actively live this Third Petition. His call comes, not with a roll of drums but through His staccato Word. And we are empowered, not with cannon and munitions but with the Word and the Spirit, to share God's will with this frail earth. We begin with prayer, but then we must act.

Sound the tattoo! Roll the drums! Enlist all over again in the army of the faithful to bring love to this loveless age, and the Gospel to this secularized era.

GIVE US
THIS DAY
OUR DAILY
BREAD

GIVE US THIS DAY
OUR DAILY BREAD

If Tom Canty, the pauper in Mark Twain's *The Prince and the Pauper,* ever prayed the Lord's Prayer, he would have prayed this petition differently from his look-alike, Edward Tudor, Prince of Wales, and heir apparent to the throne of England. He was the "Prince of Limitless Plenty," as Twain terms this son of King Henry VIII. Tom Canty, on the other hand, was the "Prince of Pauperdom."[1] He went to bed hungry and arose hungry. He scarcely knew what bread was, while the Crown Prince knew a dozen different kinds of bread and a thousand different menus with which to eat it. When their roles changed, their understanding undoubtedly did too.

In this Fourth Petition, we admit more than God's creation; we confess our desperate dependence on Him whom we dare to address as "Father" to fulfill creation's every need. A prayer from *The Imitation of Christ* begins, "Suffer me not to go away from Thee hungry and dry."[2]

We pray this petition, not in the singular of *I* or *me*, but in the plural of *us* and *our*. We do this so that we never become princes without a conscious recognition of the paupers among us, nor that we become so ingrained in physical, economic, and spiritual poverty ourselves that we never look to Him who is our Prince, Jesus

Christ, for bread that nurtures body, mind, and spirit.

THE USE OF GOD'S GIFTS

"Give us ...," we say in this petition, "give us bread!" Giving is what God does. Paul wrote, "He who supplies seed to the sower and bread for food will also supply and increase your store of seed and will enlarge the harvest of your righteousness" (2 Cor. 9:10).

Bread, and all that it symbolizes, is a gift. Prince Edward, masquerading as a pauper and beggar, discovered how rich a gift is bread. What he had taken for granted before he mistakenly ventured out of the palace as a beggar became apparent in the days he wandered around England as the identical duplicate of John Canty's son. As son of Henry VIII, he never needed to pray for bread—nor any gift. It was all his.

Edward learned, however, that the "us" and "our" of the Fourth Petition means a gift jointly to be shared rather than selfishly hoarded by one while others starve. Everett Fullam reminds us that the petition begins with "give," a carefully chosen word of the Lord "to teach us that the Lord God is the sole source of supply of everything we need."[3] Thereby we are reminded that the gift is one to be universally shared, for God is the creator of us all.

There are countless starving paupers in this world, not just the one in Mark Twain's fiction. They exist in the hundreds of thousands and tens of millions across this globe. In the Orient, rice may be their bread; in Africa, mangoes. Yet they, too, require their local variant of "bread" to survive. Thousands of helpless children die daily in the drought regions of Africa and the poverty ghettos of Latin America. In the film "Thunderheart," an FBI agent, touring a South Dakota Indian Reservation, is appalled by what he sees. He gasps that the Third World exists right in America. I don't know where he's been. There is hardly a hamlet in this country without its zone of poverty. You and I do well to share the generosity of God with the impoverished and hungering masses here and elsewhere.

THE GIFT OF BREAD

God gives us far more than bread. Luther says the term symbolizes "everything needed in life ... food and clothing, home and property, work and income, a devoted family, an orderly community, good government, favorable weather, peace and health, a good name, and true friends and neighbors."[4] In short, "bread" encompasses all our material needs.

Jan Milic Lochman entitles this aspect of the prayer as "holy materialism." Jesus' initial use of "bread" refers to the staple of life made from the commonly-harvested grain. Second, His use means nourishment in general; therefore, all that we need to eat to be healthy is found in the term. And third, Jesus' term "bread" symbolizes the heavenly bread of that eternal banquet that is before us. But fourth, by its use, Jesus also meant the bread of Holy Communion. From earliest times, the Lord's Prayer always accompanied the words of institution in the celebration of the Lord's Supper.[5] Thus, this term Jesus used has a multi-dimensional meaning.

Conversely, James Kallas writes that "hunger is the

word of Satan. Where Satan is, there is no bread ... but where God rules there is no hunger; there is food in abundance." Kallas calls our attention to the imagery in the book of Revelation. Satan is destroyed (Rev. 20), and the instantaneous outcome is the emergence of the tree that miraculously provides abundant food in all seasons. Adds Kallas, "Until 'Thy kingdom comes' and 'Thy will be done on earth as it is in heaven'—until then, hunger is a demonic fact. In the future, there will be bread in abundance, but now under Satan there is famine. Thus Jesus prays that the elect might receive in advance some of this forthcoming food, that they might even now have this bread of the future, to sustain them in the present evil age."[6]

There is a poignant scene in Alexander Solzhenitsyn's memorable novel of prison life in the Stalinist era in the Soviet Union. In *One Day in the Life of Ivan Denisovich*, prisoners in the Gulag are chatting before bedtime. Alyosha the Baptist is being taunted by less demonstrative believers, who pray from time to time and make the sign of the cross. Alyosha encourages them to pray and to pray properly. "One must never stop praying. If you have real faith, you tell a mountain to move and it will move."

"I've never seen a mountain move," responds Ivan. In fact, he had never even seen a mountain. He chides Alyosha that, for all his praying, he and his Baptist Society were all arrested and given 25 years in the labor camps, and yet they had not succeeded in making a mountain move.

"Oh, we didn't pray for that, Ivan Denisovich," responds the Baptist. "Of all earthly and mortal things, our Lord commanded us to pray only for our daily bread. 'Give us this day our daily bread.' "[7]

When the children of Israel exited Egypt in search of the Promised Land, they had no grain with which to make bread. God gave them manna. In Hebrew it is two words, *man hu*, which literally asks the question, "What is it," because the Israelites had never seen it before. Despite God's goodness, the Israelites stopped thanking God for His gift. Second, they asked no further provisions from Him. Third, says R. C. Sproul, they grumbled; and at last, they recalled the good old days in Egypt, where they had plentiful vegetables and fruits and grains to eat ... never remembering their enslavement, their bitterly oppressive state, and utter unhappiness.[8] In the Lord's Prayer we pray that we never forget the gift or the giver.

Jesus observed, "Our forefathers ate the manna in the desert; as it is written: 'He gave them bread from heaven to eat.' Jesus said to them, 'I tell you the truth, it is not Moses who has given you the bread from heaven, but it is My Father who gives you the true bread from heaven. For the bread of God is He who comes down from heaven and gives life to the world.' 'Sir,' they said, 'from now on give us this bread.' Then Jesus declared, 'I am the bread of life. He who comes to Me will never go hungry, and he who believes in Me will never be thirsty' " (John 6:31–35).

Jesus, who was born in Bethlehem, a name that means "House of Bread," and who became for us the living bread of life (John 6:51), knew how hungry people were for bread. He fed thousands with a few loaves— twice (John 6:5–13; Matt. 15:32–38). The devil tempted

Him to turn stone into bread, but Jesus refused, saying, "Man does not live on bread alone, but on every word that comes from the mouth of God" (Matt. 4:3). On Maundy Thursday He identified His betrayer by having Judas dip bread into the bowl with Him (Mark 14:20–21)—and then used bread from that same meal to institute His Holy Supper (14:22). On Easter night, after His resurrection from the grave, the Emmaus pilgrims recognized Jesus in the breaking of bread (Luke 24:28–35). On the shore of the Sea of Galilee, the disciples realized it was the risen Savior who had prepared breakfast for them of broiled fish and fresh bread (John 21:1–14).

Remembering all these events, how can we not be aware, even in our casual eating of bread and use of all His blessings, that God Himself is present among us? God provides us with the abundance of love that His giving requires. It is not only a loaf that He gives, but sliced and enriched as well. That's what we confess by "bread."

THE FREQUENCY OF BREAD

We are told that the starving children of World War II would not go to sleep unless a piece of bread rested on their pillow.[9] Mark Twain's fictional Prince of Wales never had to worry about a crust of bread—until he switched places with Tom Canty. Then he learned that the word *daily* has meaning.

The word Jesus uses here for "daily" is unique. It is not found anywhere in classical or New Testament Greek. Some people thought Matthew made up the word—that is, until 1947, when they unearthed the Dead Sea scrolls. Among all the shards of pottery and scraps of papyrus and parchment was a shopping list—and Jesus' word was on the list. It was the designation of a category: the items a housewife needed to purchase every day in the *agora*, the marketplace. A recently-found, fifth-century Egyptian papyrus also uses the term on a list of expenses to identify "a daily ration."[10]

The emphasis in on the daily reception of that which cannot be stored up for the future. Barclay words the thought in this way: "[The petition] teaches us to live one day at a time, and not to worry and be anxious about the distant and the unknown future."[11]

Jesus Himself is the best example of this aspect of the prayer. After He left carpentry and began wandering the countryside as an itinerant rabbi, He had to depend on the kindness of strangers. Even when He lived in Capernaum, His daily bread was not something He Himself grew, harvested, ground into flour, kneaded, and baked; it came from the caring hands of others. Yet He cheerfully went about His business of preaching the Good News, despite His dependence on others for His daily bread. He knew the Father would supply it—and He did.

A member of my former parish found a horn of plenty in the dumpsters of his apartment complex: he salvages the throw-aways of others and gives them to the needy. Another former parishioner who was in utter poverty always had a cheerful smile as she spoke about her widow's jar (a reference to the never-empty jar of flour Elijah provided the widow of Zarephath, 1 Kings 17:8–16). Daily, this parishioner went in prayer to the

Lord for her needs that day—and daily it was provided! She was astounded. I was shocked. But it happened. She trusted God and He never failed her.

Although you and I might not have similar, fantastic accounts to relate, we can still truthfully confess that God provides for us daily—just as we pray.

MORE THAN CRUMBS

The gift and the Giver are identified in this petition. We receive bread for food and living bread from heaven—daily. They are supplied to us by the God whose love knows no limits. He sanctifies material needs and blesses the receivers, but He still makes us a family by encouraging us to address Him as Father and insisting that we pray for "us" and "our" needs together. This prayer is so simple that children easily memorize it, yet so amply filled that its profound ideas require a lifetime of exploring, says Steve Harper.[12] "Give us this day our daily bread" is not an idle comment, glibly to be recited, but an important petition faithfully to be confessed.

He offers us more than crumbs, but bread. Savor it. It is good to taste and marvelous to share.

FORGIVE US OUR TRESPASSES, AS WE FORGIVE THOSE WHO TRESPASS AGAINST US

FORGIVE US OUR TRESPASSES, AS WE FORGIVE THOSE WHO TRESPASS AGAINST US

In the Middle East the melting snow of Mount Hermon forms the source for several streams that eventually comprise the Jordan River. Despite impediments along the way, the water flows southward, forming a small lake called Huleh (now turned into farmland), and then the larger lake we know as the Sea of Galilee. The Jordan pushes further southward along the Asian-African Rift until it dead-ends in the Dead Sea. Unable to penetrate through the Negev Desert to the Gulf of Aqabah, it dies.

God's forgiving grace is like an immense reservoir high in the altitude of the heavenly reaches. We, however, live in this world, which we may depict as an arid wasteland of sin that, like the area of the Dead Sea, is far below sea level—and a million miles beneath the heaven of heavens. The refreshing water of Grace Lake has an outlet that cascades bountifully downward toward us; but artificial dams of resentment, unforgiveness, anger, and anxiety have been erected along the way, so that its flow is often less than a trickle and may not get through to others. We gasp dry-mouthed and thirsty, like wanderers in the Sahara looking for an oasis, when all we need to do is destroy the dams we ourselves have erected between God's plentiful forgiveness and our desperate need to quench our craving for pardon's refreshment. When forgiveness is unable to penetrate the arid wasteland of pride and animosity, relationships die.

At the conclusion of the prayer in Matthew, the Lord Jesus explains this petition's implications in precise language. He says, "For if you forgive others their trespasses, your heavenly Father will also forgive you; but if you do not forgive others, neither will your Father forgive your trespasses" (6:14–15 NRSV). It's almost as if God is pushing grace down a hill to all; it flows from God Himself, through us, to those who offend us. This petition turns the whole prayer around from solely God's action to our own willingly confessed involvement: living in forgiveness.

By God working in us, this petition is meant to make couples indissoluble and to mend family rifts, to end rivalries, vengeance, vendettas, and spats. It is intended to reconcile the separated and unite the scattered, to make angry neighbors friends again. It is a petition to end hostilities, to squelch violence, and to open folded arms of dissatisfaction in order to welcome home estranged brothers and sisters. Such is the act of grace and the art of forgiveness.

FORGIVING GRACE AS AN INEXHAUSTIBLE RESERVOIR

Grace is like that vast lake in the mountains, crystal clear, shimmering in the golden sunshine, and as pure as melted snow can be, unadulterated and uncontaminated. Grace Lake, however, is oceanic in size; it is unlimited, for no drought can empty it, nor can any thirst dry it up. Hear the way God describes it. "From His fullness we have all received, grace upon grace" (John 1:16 NRSV); it "overflow[s] to the many" (Rom. 5:15); it's an "abundant provision" (5:17); it's "surpassing" (2 Cor. 9:14); it's "sufficient" (12:9); it possesses "incomparable riches" (Eph. 2:7); and it "was poured out ... abundantly" (1 Tim. 1:14), "for the grace of God that brings salvation has appeared to all men" (Titus 2:11).

This vast sea of grace came into being because Jesus, lifted upon the towering cross of Calvary, lovingly gave His life for you and me and everyone everywhere for all time—for our worst enemy as well as our best friend, for our greatest foes as well as our dearest neighbors. It is not a hidden sea, this ocean of forgiveness. We know where it is and how to receive its life-giving waters. All we need do is ask for it; and, in Christ's name and because of Jesus' triumph, it is ours. And once ours, God intends His grace to journey through us peacefully.

OBSTRUCTING THE FLOW OF GRACE

The Negev Desert and its mountain ranges, higher than the Dead Sea, impede the southward thrust of the Jordan River to the Gulf of Aqabah. Similarly, people unwilling to live in forgiveness impede the flow of grace, so that it never dampens the toe of many. It is not that God is withdrawing His forgiving grace from the unforgiving; rather, we are erecting dams more eagerly than beavers or allowing deserts to blow higher than the flow of the river of grace. Love in the form of forgiving

91

grace must be let loose lest it die.

When King Frederick William I of Prussia lay dying, he was forewarned by his pastor that he must forgive all his enemies—including George II of England, his brother-in-law, whom he hated most. Reluctantly, Frederick told his wife, "Write to your brother and tell him I forgive him, but be sure not to do it until after my death."

Madame Defarge, the villainess of Charles Dickens' *A Tale of Two Cities,* is one of the most vengeful people in all of English literature. As a child, she had been wronged by the aristocratic Evremonde brothers, who brutally mistreated her peasant family. Over the years, she had built so many dams of hateful resentment and had established so many deserts of bitterness that they formed an impenetrable barrier even to the brothers' innocent heirs, who never wronged her in any way. Wrote Dickens, "But, imbued from her childhood with a brooding sense of wrong, and an inveterate hatred of a class, opportunity had developed her into a tigress. She was absolutely without pity. If she had ever had the virtue in her, it had quite gone out of her."[1]

For such people, Jesus said, "For if you forgive others their trespasses, your heavenly Father will also forgive you; but if you do not forgive others, neither will your Father forgive your trespasses" (Matt. 6:14–15 NRSV). It is not that He won't; He can't. The means of flow is blocked, not by Him but by us. Guilt, animosity, hatred, vengeance—these boulders form massive and impenetrable barriers, huge walls of resentment, and stop the rapid stream of grace from flowing onward.

When we reject forgiveness as appropriate for others, we're rejecting it as appropriate for all people, including ourselves. We are rejecting our own forgiveness in Christ—and our relationship is allowed to become a Dead Sea.

In Jesus' parable of the unforgiving servant (Matt. 18:23–35), a former slave owed his employer a huge sum of money and could not pay it back. The employer ordered the man sold, together with his wife and children (an acceptable way to deal with deadbeats in those days). The servant pleaded with his employer, vowing to pay back everything. The employer, touched by the man's pathetic entreaty, not only forgave him the entire debt, but released him as well from his imprisonment.

This man, who had received so much, was not the least bit charitable to a third man, who owed him a great deal less—only 100 denarii compared to 10,000 talents (akin to $1,000 compared to $10 million). This third man was thrown into debtors' prison until he could settle the debt. When the employer discovered the former slave's brutal behavior, he scolded him, "I canceled all that debt of yours because you begged me to. Shouldn't have had mercy on your fellow servant just as I had on you?" Then the unmerciful servant was handed over to the authorities to be tortured until he would pay his entire debt. Jesus summarizes by saying, "This is how My heavenly Father will treat each of you unless you forgive your brother from your heart" (v. 35).

The parable was Jesus' answer to Peter's timeless question about the extent of mercy: should I forgive as many as seven times? You know the Lord's response: "Not seven times, but 77 times" (Matt. 18:21–23).

C. S. Lewis reminds us that to forgive for the moment is not the problem. "But to go on forgiving, to forgive the same offense again every time it recurs to the memory—there's the real tussle."[2]

Luther says, "The love among Christians should be the same kind of love as that of every member of the body for every other one, as St. Paul often says (Rom. 12:4–5; 1 Cor. 12:12–26), each one accepting the faults of the other, sympathizing with them, bearing and removing them, and doing everything possible to help him. Hence the doctrine of forgiveness of sins is the most important of all, both for us personally and for our relations with others. As Christ continually bears with us in His kingdom and forgives us all sorts of faults, so we should bear and forgive one another in every situation and in every way." Luther made this observation on the basis of his exposition of Matthew 5:32 that deals with divorce.[3] If we're honest with one another, we'll agree that lack or withholding of forgiveness, or even the refusal to be forgiven, is what breaks once-tight families into fragments. It can even break apart the family of the church.

One pastor, upset that members were leaving his parish for another, called the other pastor and berated him. When he was told that those who were switching were people battered by personal tragedy, broken and beaten down by life's squeeze plays, people who needed a new starting place, the original pastor shouted, "You're nothing but a bunch of garbage collectors." He saw those people as refuse!

When the accused pastor mentioned this to a group of parishioners, one of them spoke up. "Let me tell you something about garbage," he said, mentioning a former landfill not far from the church. "For ten years we used it as a place to dump trash and garbage. Know what's there now? A beautiful park."[4] People too can go from garbage to gardens. Forgiveness turns trashy relationships into treasured ones; going from refuse to a refusion of former enemies into oneness.

Ron Davis told the above story in a chapter entitled "The Fellowship of the Forgiven." That's an apt title, for the church is a fellowship community where the dams are removed, the avalanches scooped away, the desert barriers removed, and God's grace is allowed to flow unimpeded from the reservoir of Christ's love. Paul put it in frank terms: "Bear with each other and forgive whatever grievances you may have against one another. Forgive as the Lord forgave you" (Col. 3:13).

REMOVING THE BARRIERS

That which flushes aside the resentment and the anger that clogs up the river of love is forgiveness. It's gained by confession. It's set free by dislodging guilt. It flushes out rumor, misunderstanding, gossip, and grouchiness. It's built by engineering sin out of the way. We need to be like Ferdinand de Lesseps and push our Suez Canal through impediments to the other end. When God's people engineer away impediments from the free flow of the river of grace, then grow the flowers of friendship amid the companionship of neighbors.

How do we do this? We begin by recanting the situation. We repent that a division has come between two former friends. We resolve to heal it. If the other party won't come to us, we go to them. In the process, we discover enmity dislodged, and the smooth flow of grace returns. If the other party is unwilling, we nevertheless know that we have done our utmost to unclog love's pipeline.

A number of years ago, a family was split. The only daughter had fallen in love with a man of dubious character. Her upset parents forbade her to continue to see the young man. In a fit of youthful passion, she ran off with him, 500 miles away, vowing never to see her parents again. But the daughter was too precious to the parents to allow that to happen. By some careful investigating, they found out where she was, and the dad and I sped over the freeways one night from Sacramento to the Los Angeles Basin. It was not to retrieve the daughter, but to repair the damaged relationship. Only when her father sought forgiveness for his strident charges and apologized for the way he acted did she realize forgiveness needed to flow both ways. She, too, repented—and suddenly the flood of grace engulfed them both as the final dam was erased from the clogged waterway of love.

An American pastor headed a committee in Switzerland early in this century. There was a disagreement between the director and his committee, so they dismissed him. Going into a nearby chapel for solitude and prayer, the former director decided (says Paul Tournier in his book *Creative Suffering*) not only to forgive the committee members for their action, but, through personal letters, to recognize his own complicity and seek their forgiveness for it. Dr. Tournier says it takes courage to ask for forgiveness.[5] I say it takes common sense—and faith in the Christ who said of His crucifiers, "Father, forgive them ..." (Luke 23:34).

One of the greatest preachers of the 20th century, Paul Tillich, published a sermon entitled "To Whom Much Is Forgiven ...," which says, "Forgiveness is unconditional or it is not forgiveness at all .... Genuine forgiveness is participation, reunion overcoming the powers of estrangement. ... We cannot love unless we have accepted forgiveness, and the deeper our experience of forgiveness is, the greater is our love."[6] That's what brings into being the "Fellowship of the Forgiven."

Paul has given us a practical way to flush out the sins that clog God's river of grace. "Get rid of all bitterness, rage and anger, brawling and slander, along with every form of malice. Be kind and compassionate to one another, forgiving each other, just as in Christ God forgave you. Be imitators of God, therefore, as dearly loved children and live a life of love, just as Christ loved us and gave Himself up for us as a fragrant offering and sacrifice to God" (Eph. 4:31–5:2). We begin by putting away the resentments and cultivating the essentials for renewing friendship.

The Final Product

We've talked of that gigantic, heavenly sea of grace and the inhibiting deserts of resentment as well as the excavation tools and flushing agents of Christian forgiveness. Now we must examine the final product. What happens when grace flows through you and me into those around us?

Isn't there joy, or something close to it? Perhaps even ecstasy? Martin Luther says that the forgiving person "will rejoice in the opening of the way to forgiveness." Alvin Rogness says of the potential forgiver, "Not until he is made whole in God will he know peace and freedom."[7] Then celebration explodes in a spiritual display of happy internal fireworks. There is the joy of liberation from the debt of the old sin, from the penalty of the old trespass, and reunion results.

But what do we do with the old remnants of separation? We need to put away the remembrance of the heartache and, in its place, put the memory of reconciliation. Remember the lesson learned, but no longer relive the agony. You've given it away to God in Christ, who gives you back the peace that surpasses understanding (Phil. 4:7). There no longer exists the no-man's land of indifference, nor have you a need for white flags of defeat or red flags of battle. The surrender has been made; and wholeness, the new creation that God creates, wears the colors of joy.

Thomas Watson points out that Jesus provides us but one petition for the body: "Give us this day our daily bread," but three for the soul: "Forgive us our trespasses," "Lead us not into temptation," and "Deliver us from evil." Continues Watson, "Observe hence, that we are to be more careful for our souls than for our bodies; more careful for grace than for daily bread; and more desirous to have our souls saved than our bodies fed."[8]

This, then, is the pivotal petition of the prayer, the one that involves us directly, that implores us to live in forgiveness. Let grace flow by letting go of resentment. Watch the dams burst, and the grace of God will drench you with such refreshing joy that you will know again the powerful wonder of forgiveness.

LEAD US NOT INTO TEMPTATION, BUT DELIVER US FROM EVIL

Lead Us Not into Temptation, but Deliver Us from Evil

Balaam, a Mesopotamian soothsayer, was on his way to see the king of Moab, who had summoned him. The king, worried over the Israelites encamped on his territory, wanted a curse to be put on them. As Balaam went to the palace of the king, his donkey saw what Balaam could not: the angel of the Lord. So the animal went around it, off the path. Balaam beat the beast for its obstinate behavior. It happened a second time, and there was a second beating. "Then," says the book of Numbers, "the angel of the LORD moved on ahead and stood in a narrow place where there was no room to turn, either to the right or to the left" (22:26). The donkey lay down and angered its master all the more, until finally the beast spoke and let Balaam in on the cause. Then Balaam saw the angel himself—and discovered what we all can find: "God in the narrow places," as Methodist Bishop Gerald Kennedy puts it. "How many times," he observes, "we find that in such a place is where God meets us,"[1] between the rock of temptation and the hard place of evil, a narrow spot of testing.

Abraham, too, journeyed to the narrow spot of testing (Gen. 22:1–19). God had ordered the patriarch to sacrifice his son, his only son Isaac, whom he truly loved.

Abraham was plunged into the most difficult test possible, an ancient "Sophie's Choice," only it was not a choice between two children, but the choice between doing what God said or disobeying Him. As Abraham built the altar, readied the firewood, and was ready to do that horrible deed, the angel who stood in the narrow way of Balaam's travels withheld Abraham's hand, and a ram caught in a nearby thicket was sacrificed instead. Satan must have been surprised to find that God's faithful people, plunged into the narrow places of life, do more than survive; they trust God and He does not fail them. (We can only wonder what Satan thought for a brief moment when the Father did not do the same for His own Son, but gave Him up for all.)

The intent of the Lord's Prayer is to ready disciples for difficulty, for persecution and turmoil, for a journey through life that is not always a smooth freeway, but bumpy, pothole-filled, and dangerous. "By flight alone we cannot overcome," writes an ancient theologian, "but by patience and true humility we become stronger than all our enemies"—and happier, I would add. Discovering God in the constricted passage between temptation and evil is a moment of joy in the journey.

TEMPTATION AS TEST AND TRIAL

Although in traditional English we pray "Lead us not into temptation," the apostle James explains, "When tempted, no one should say, 'God is tempting me.' For God cannot be tempted by evil, nor does He tempt anyone; but each one is tempted when, by his own evil desire, he is dragged away and enticed" (1:13–14). Why, then, pray that God refrain from leading us somewhere He won't take us to begin with?

The Greek word Jesus uses for "temptation," *peirasmon*, means something other than being lured into sin. While it can have that connotation, Kenneth Leech assures us "the language conveys a stronger meaning. Biblical writers did not think much in terms of inner struggles between right and wrong, but in more concrete terms of 'testing' and 'trial.'" Says William Barclay, "In its New Testament usage, to *tempt* a person is not so much to seek to seduce him into sin, as it is to test his strength and his loyalty and his ability for service."[2]

When we think of such testing, the biblical example of Abraham's near sacrifice of Isaac quickly comes to mind—along with the very human amazement, "How could any father have had such faith? I could never survive such a test." Aware of his own weaknesses, the author of Proverbs 30:8–9 wrote, "Give me neither poverty nor riches, ... Otherwise, I may have too much and disown You .... Or I may become poor and steal, and so dishonor the name of my God." Therefore, we pray to our Father, that He would keep us from those trials and tests which our faith might not survive. While Revelation 7:14 speaks of those who have come out of the great tribulation, St. John clearly implies that others did not. The "temptation" of the Sixth Petition refers to more than just everyday enticements, it acknowledges our ultimate, eschatological testing.

It is this kind of trial, this kind of test, that Jesus had in mind when He taught His disciples to pray this brief but consoling prayer. He knew the way ahead would be rough; thus He reminded us to deny ourselves, take up our crosses daily, and follow Him (Luke 9:23). After all, He says, "No one comes to the Father except through Me" (John 14:6).

This is not to say that we automatically will fail such tests. After all, St. Peter wrote that trials "have come so that your faith—of greater worth than gold, which perishes even though refined by fire—may be proved genuine and may result in praise, glory and honor when Jesus Christ is revealed" (1 Peter 1:7). But we dare not underestimate such trials, nor think that we, by ourselves, can overcome them. As John Knox reminds us, "Christ Jesus has fought our battle, He Himself has taken us under His care and protection; however violently the Devil may tempt us, by temptations spiritual or physical, he is not able to pluck us out of the hand of the potent Son of God."[3]

Though the petition prays primarily about the ultimate test, we are not wrong to use this petition to ask our Father to help us in the daily temptations to yield to sin. Paul sent Timothy to Thessalonica to minister to the Christians there, "to strengthen and encourage [them] for the sake of [their] faith, so that no one would be shaken by these persecutions" (1 Thess. 3:2–3 NRSV)—persecutions that come precisely because of the Christians' faith.

More recently, Nien Cheng, in her best-selling autobiography, wrote about persecution she met as a Christian in China. "Throughout the [six-and-a-half] years of my imprisonment, I had turned to God often and felt His presence. ... My faith had sustained me in these the darkest hours of my life and brought me safely through privation, sickness, and torture. At the same time, my suffering had strengthened my faith and made me realize that God was always there."[4] She prayed with her head bent over a copy of Mao Zedong's book, because she could not pray openly in the prison where she was confined. She found hope in a time of persecution.

Solzhenitsyn, who wrote about Baptist Alyosha praying under the duress of prison life, drew on his own experiences of imprisonment, when prayer offered hope in a terror-ridden time of trial.[5]

So too, Pavel Uhorskai, a Lutheran pastor in former Czechoslovakia, lived out some of his persecution in a Communist prison, from 1949–53. At his trial, a Communist agent commented angrily, "I suppose ... you want to distort Marxist-Leninism ... to fight against us." They asked if he had any weapons. Finally Uhorskai showed them his Bible and answered, "Yes, I have this one." They asked no further questions about weapons.[6]

A certain man named Basil, a Russian Christian, spent 10 years in a labor camp for publishing Christian tracts. He discovered, however, that he could preach in prison in the few minutes between the time the prisoners assembled in the morning to be counted and the guards came out to check on them. It took him two weeks to preach one sermon, but he did it.[7]

In North America we are not tormented by government policy to relinquish our faith, but we are tempted by society's norms and political correctness to keep silent about our Lord and how our lives have changed because of Him—and especially about how He can change the lives of others. Therefore, just as the promise held true for the saints and martyrs of old as well as the

Chengs, Solzhenitsyns, and Uhorskais of today, so the promise is ours: "No testing has overtaken you that is not common to everyone. God is faithful, and He will not let you be tested beyond your strength, but with the testing He will also provide the way out so that you may be able to endure it" (1 Cor. 10:13 NRSV).

Trials and tests, terrors and temptations, for today as well as the Last Day—these are what we pray God to lead us successfully to avoid.

THE TEMPTER AND DEVILISH TERROR

In the petition about bread, we deal with the present; in the petition concerning forgiveness, we deal with the past; but in these two petitions that confront testing and trials as well as out-and-out evil, we look to an uncertain future in this life.[8] We seek release from trials and testings; and, in the Seventh Petition (which only Matthew records), we implore God to deliver us from evil, that is, the Evil One, for the evil in this world has a source.

Dr. D. Martyn Lloyd-Jones, pastor of London's famed Westminster Chapel, explains, "This world is governed by a power that is inimical to God. He is described as 'the god of this world' or 'Satan,' and he has organized his forces with such unusual ability and power and subtlety that everything in this life and the world is set against God's people. Temptations, suggestions, insinuations, the whole outlook, the whole bias— I need not describe them, they are all against us."[9] This is the role of the tempter.

Satan's evil manifests itself in every kind of horror

and every conceivable terror. It can be physical illness or economic upheaval or political chaos. It can be drugs and drink, abused sex, maltreated workers, corruption in government, mayhem in the neighborhood, wrong-headed thinking, trashy publications, inane films, abject poverty, gross ignorance, ignored and alienated children—the list can go on and on, from human arrogance to inhuman action or inaction. Satan is the purveyor of all that's evil. Thus we pray that we may be delivered from his most heinous evil, from hell itself, and hellishness here.

Not only do we pray this, but we also live it, confessing by our actions that, in Jesus the Lord, we wrestle triumphantly with Satan. How do we do this? By imitating our Lord's own battle in the wilderness with the conniving devil (Matt. 4:1–11; Mark 1:12–13; Luke 4:1–13). "Humble yourselves, therefore, under God's mighty hand," advises the apostle Peter "that He may lift you up in due time. Cast all your anxiety on [Jesus] because He cares for you. Be self-controlled and alert. Your enemy the devil prowls around like a roaring lion looking for someone to devour. Resist him, standing firm in the faith, because you know that your brothers throughout the world are undergoing the same kind of suffering" (1 Peter 5:6–9).

St. Paul counsels, "Finally, be strong in the Lord and in His mighty power. Put on the full armor of God so that you can take your stand against the devil's schemes. For our struggle is not against flesh and blood, but against the rulers, against the authorities, against the powers of this dark world and against the spiritual forces of evil in the heavenly realms. Therefore put on the full armor of God, so that when the day of evil comes, you may be able to stand your ground, and after you have done everything, to stand' (Eph. 6:10–13). It is when we put on the whole armor of faith that we have no fear about the future destiny, about trials and tribulations, tests and tempests. Those who hold on to Christ hang on to God's promises. Those who meet life's storms with God's Gospel ringing in their ears and hearts will not falter.

D. Martyn Lloyd-Jones calls this "the doctrine of the final perseverance of the saints." He says, "It was the doctrine that sustained the saints of the New Testament era . . . and since that time there has been nothing that has so held and stimulated God's people."[10] He says that this doctrine explains the great exploits of simple Christians when they were caught in life's storms. They met overwhelming opposition, knowing God would not abandon them. They remembered Jesus' words, "I give them eternal life, and they shall never perish; no one can snatch them out of My hand" (John 10:28–29).

That's the way to live out these petitions and leave the tempter as exasperated as when he battled Jesus in the wilderness of the Jordan and found himself wounded by the Lord's denial of both his power and his will—and then found himself mortally afflicted, when Jesus made a conquest of death and the grave on Calvary's hill and Easter's dawn.

THE TEMPESTS OF LIFE

Satan is his name; temptation is his game. His intention is so to engage us in the terror of a tempest that we deny the very one who quiets swirling seas and storm-force winds with the word "peace" (Mark 4:35–41).

Our journey in life is not always a peaceful drive along shaded lanes with a cloudless sky and a bright sun. We're often caught in emotional gusty squalls or spiritual drenching downpours. Life is not free of storms; blizzard conditions seem to immobilize us. Yet we can have sunshine in the soul.

As we pray these petitions, "Lead us not into temptation, but deliver us from evil," let God scatter the fearsome clouds and, through His Word, give you His umbrella of blessing and the joyous burst of renewing sunshine.

Here is certainty on which to depend regardless of the gale force winds and the deluge. In Christ the storm is stilled.

Our journey, remember, is with Christ at the lead, who squeezes us through the narrow places more easily than the broad ways that lead to destruction (Matt. 7:13–14). Yield to no one else, but Him.

THINE IS THE KINGDOM AND THE POWER AND THE GLORY FOREVER AND EVER AMEN

Thine Is the Kingdom and the Power and the Glory Forever and Ever. Amen.

To the accompaniment of applause, the conductor enters the stage and briskly mounts the platform. With his upraised hands, the alert musicians are poised to respond immediately. Then a prompt downbeat comes, and the rich music of a symphony erupts as gracefully as a rose unfolding, the strings singing the theme. The mellow sounds of the cello, the deep resonance of the double bass, and the smooth song of the violas blend with the violins, as the woodwinds, brass, and percussion instruments support the ethereal melody. In movement after movement, various themes wed differing concepts, so that at the end, when the symphony is concluding, a coda or some other recapitulation enthusiastically summarizes what has been played.

What a metaphor for the Lord's Prayer! With praise in the words and ecstasy in the phrasing, the doxology joyously acclaims all that has been said in the petitions and affirms Him who gave this prayer to His people.

We should not be dismayed that the earliest copies of Matthew and Luke do not include these doxological words of the Lord's Prayer. (Of 6,000 New Testament fragments or whole manuscripts from early centuries, only about half contain it in part or total.) They were added in their entirety perhaps before the end of the second century. But, as Everett Fullam says, "If Jesus didn't say it, He very well could have, because it harmonizes perfectly with what we have already examined and brings the prayer full circle."[1]

Christians who conclude this masterful prayer with the doxology do so with reason. "Doxology" comes from two Greek words: *doxa*, which means "praise," and *legein*, "speak." A doxology is an appendage that adds deliberate praise. As Girgensohn explains, "The Christian church took over from Old Testament and synagogue worship the custom of closing all public prayers with an ascription of praise to God." Similarly, whenever Christians sang or said the psalms, they usually added a Christian doxology, the *Gloria Patri*, "Glory be to the Father, and to the Son, and to the Holy Spirit ...."[2] It distinguished Christianity's interpretation of the Old Testament psalms from their origin in Judaism. This doxology added to the Lord's Prayer follows that tradition.

We know that a form of the doxology was used early in the Christian church, for one appears in the ancient writing known as "The Teaching of the Twelve Apostles," or, as it is best known, the *Didache* (from the end of the first century).[3] The doxology has its origin in the words of 1 Chronicles 29:10–11; thus it is biblical, while also being an appropriate summation of Jesus' prayer. It is truly a hymn of praise, a brief but grand recapitulation of the themes Jesus included and a wonderful ending to an absolutely ageless prayer that is to the Christian's heart a celebrative symphony of hope.

To confess this prayer and to live its doxology—these are the challenges before us. It seems to me, Paul suggests how in his letter to the Colossians, when he prayed that they might be "strengthened with all power according to His glorious might so that you may have great endurance and patience, and joyfully giving thanks to the Father, who has qualified you to share in the inheritance of the saints in the kingdom of light. For He has rescued us from the dominion of darkness and brought us into the kingdom of the Son He loves, in whom we have redemption, the forgiveness of sins" (1:11–14).

As we focus on how we may make this doxology a symphonic theme by which to live, consider *what* is being said, *why* it is being said, and *by whom and to whom* it is addressed.

WHAT WE'RE PRAISING

In this summary to the Lord's Prayer, we speak of the *kingdom* (referring back to the Second Petition), God's rule in heaven and on earth as well as in the hearts of His believers. We refer to the *power*, manifest in the God who can will things to be done in heaven and on earth, as well as provide bread, forgive sin, and preserve us from both the time of trial and the tempter of evil (Petitions Three through Seven). God's *glory* (from the First Petition) is in who He is—which includes His hallowed name as well as His hallowed being and the hallowed relationship we have with Him, for He is our

Father. Thus, what is being said in the doxology recapitulates the prayer's seven essential parts in three remarkable words.

The gifted English writer C. S. Lewis penned to a friend his understanding of these words in the doxology. "I have an idea of the *kingdom* as sovereignty *de jure*; God, as good, would have a claim on my obedience even if He had no power. The *power* is the sovereignty *de facto*—He is omnipotent. And the *glory* is—well, the glory; the 'beauty so old and new,' the 'light from behind the sun.' "[4]

Yet the final word has not been heard: Amen! It is the resounding affirmation of God, who is "forever and ever," as well as of the believer. Martin Luther teaches, "We say Amen because we are certain that such petitions are pleasing to our Father in heaven and are heard by Him. For He Himself has commanded us to pray in this way and has promised to hear us."[5]

"Amen" said by God means "it is and shall be so," while its utterance by human beings indicates "so let it be."[6] It is a word of agreement that should imply that the petitioner is going to live out the agreement. Here is where the Lord's Prayer shifts from prayer to confession. Since God is God, you and I can live life more vitally. He has the power. It isn't in the hands of the affluent, nor is it in the hands of the political right or left. Real power is in His hands. You and I, living as members of His kingdom, can glorify Him by not yielding to the darker powers that seek to diminish God and erase joy. In short, we can live out the exciting affirmation of this Doxology. We can be "Amen people," affirming Christ and His Gospel and our Father, whose grace redeems us.

Joseph Haydn, the composer, said once, "God gave me a cheerful heart, so He will surely forgive me if I serve Him cheerfully."[7] All of Haydn's music is an affirming "Amen" to the Gospel's joy. Here is the secret to living the "Amen life": to live with joy, with fortitude, with delight in Him whom we praise—and do it with zest.

Why We're Praising

Jan Milic Lochman, the renown Czech theologian, believes "that in this ending we have more than pious liturgical usage. Here once again and finally, our need before God, specifically our need of prayer, is addressed and highlighted in hope."[8]

That's why the doxology is there—to give hope, to provide impetus. It's like a cheerleader, stimulating us to such excitement of faith that no enemy can defeat us, no lethargy can sweep us into the state of spiritual couch potatoes, and no impending conflict can cause us to crumble like a sand castle before a colossal wave. It's like a conductor, pulling the various instruments of a great philharmonic orchestra together to be one voice in interpreting the magnificent music of life in Christ. There is hope.

We Christians are dealing with the God who *is* God, God Almighty, the God of power and love. In a famous sermon a few years after the discovery of atomic power, Peter Marshall observed that "not a single one of the new powers discovered by man possesses any redeeming force. Neither fire, nor steam, nor explosives, nor electricity, nor atomic energy can change his nature."

Continued the beloved Presbyterian minister, "The greatest force ever bestowed on mankind streamed forth in blood and sweat and tears and death on Calvary ... when Jesus of Nazareth was crucified on the cross.

"It was a power so great that it shattered the last fortress—death. It was a power so great that it made atonement for all the sin of all the world. It was a power so great that it provided for those who would accept it the ability to live victoriously like children of God, in fellowship with Him Who made the world and the sun, the moon and the stars.

"It was power that would enable believers to do the mighty works of Christ, and to experience, flowing in and through their own lives, the energy of God.

"Here is a power so tremendous that with it nothing is impossible; and without it, nothing we do has any eternal value or significance.

"It is a power so simple that a child may use it .... Yet we reach for that power only when our hands are clasped in prayer."[9]

Thus, the doxology reminds us we are powerless, unless we are empowered by Him who is our Father, whose will controls heaven and can master the trials on earth. In that reminder we are given exceptional hope.

When we've prayed the prayer Jesus taught and have concluded with the doxology His followers added, you and I are spiritually energized to change the status quo as conduits of His love—not alone, but as the people of God, the church, His disciples who pray and believe and live out the prayer He taught us.

To Whom and
by Whom Is the Praise

Although a person alone may utter the Lord's Prayer, it is always in the plural. "We" and "us" and "our" are the pronouns used. This disciples' prayer draws together the whole family of the faithful, the early followers of Jesus with the church alive as well as with the glorified church alive in eternity. No one prays this prayer alone.

Even more wonderful, Jesus prays this prayer with us. He knows its fullness, and He seeks its completion in our lives. Even one name of the prayer, "The Our Father," reminds us that Jesus was the first to say "our" and to include Himself in it. It is truly the *Lord's* prayer, and He is present in the praying of it. "I will do whatever you ask in My Name, so that the Son may bring glory to the Father," said Jesus. "You may ask Me for anything in My name, and I will do it" (John 14:13–14).

This is what gives excitement and joy to life, for in the process of glorifying God, we discover God in Christ celebrating with us. So it is when we live this prayer, when we confess it by the lives we lead. Jesus is with us through the presence and power of the Holy Spirit. His love for us is so limitless that it does not leave us as one without a prayer partner. He affirms our praying.

Thus, pray this prayer and sing its doxology. Rejoice that you are not insignificant in His eyes, though you be one or a few, for He stands with all the saints in confessing the kingdom and the power and the glory of Him who is and always shall be, our Father, forever and ever!

DON'T MISS
MEETING THE MASTER

In the short novel *Holy Masquerade,* the agnostic wife of a pastor in a small Swedish village searches for but cannot find the intimacy she seeks with Christ. One Palm Sunday, out of duty, she attends a church service. As the pastors at the altar pray audibly the Lord's Prayer, she is suddenly mesmerized. Above the altar she sees an image, a vision of Jesus. She is both baffled by it and awed. It draws her to her feet, and this disbelieving woman moves transfixed in the direction of the altar. But her agnostic mind stops her. There is no "amen" of affirmation, no "yea, yea, it shall be so" in her soul. As quickly as the vision came, it disappears. She leaves whining, complaining, questioning, bitter.

As you pray the Lord's Prayer today, look for Jesus; but look for Him as more than a vision. Glorify Him whose power atones for our sin and enables us to be with Him forever and ever, whose love for us not only sent Him to the cross but to the triumph of Easter.

In this prayer we have a symphony of joy, a *Te Deum* of praise that rejoices in the God who wants to fellowship with His people. Here in the doxology is the amen that says it shall be so. Here is the coda that recapitulates all the themes of the Lord's own prayer in joyous praise.

In the small, bustling community of Ocean Springs, Mississippi, I came upon a rare jewel. A small museum there celebrates the work of a local artist, Walter Inglis Anderson, said to be a "mystic, poet, naturalist, and prolific artist." The man became so obsessed with the world

God created that he left family and neighbors to observe it, sketch and paint it. He so separated himself from reality that he was hospitalized for several years for Schizophrenia. But his solitary trips to Horn Island, off the Mississippi Gulf coast, and his penchant for sketching and painting have provided us a unique view of genius.

After his death in 1965, his family went to his cottage to retrieve his simple possessions. There they found one room which had become one of Walter Anderson's greatest easels. He had decorated the four walls, floor, and ceiling with a rich, vibrant scene that has been called "Creation at Sunrise." Visitors today are amazed by the symphony of color and the music of Walter Anderson's painting of praise.[10]

When the family first discovered the room in 1965, they found Anderson's Bible opened to Psalm 104. The artist had copied by hand certain passages from that glorious hymn of praise (vv. 1–5, 10–13, 16–27, and 30–35). His widow believes the room to be a painted psalm. That psalm concludes:

> May the glory of the LORD endure forever;
>   may the LORD rejoice in His works—
> He who looks at the earth, and it trembles,
>   who touches the mountains, and they smoke.
> I will sing to the LORD all my life;
>   I will sing praise to my God as long as I live.
> May my meditation be pleasing to Him,
>   as I rejoice in the LORD ....
> Praise the LORD, O my soul.
> Praise the LORD.

Here was Walter Anderson's coda, and it ministers well to the many who come to see not only "the Little Room," but his many other grand works of art that praise God from whom all blessings flow, that enunciate so distinctly "For thine is the kingdom and the power and the glory forever and ever. Amen." May our lives as well as provide a continual recapitulation of our faith as we confess the Lord's Prayer.

Epilog

Ansgar, an aged monk and an illuminator of manuscripts, was so mature in years that his beard was no longer flecked with gray nor the hue of pewter, but startlingly white. He had arthritic knees, but slender, unbothered hands. With brush and pen he labored lovingly over the manuscripts, being careful to make no mistakes. Yet his monastery, famed for the treasures from his artful hands, was deep in debt. Sales were off. Manuscripts, hand done and beautiful, were not selling.

Brother Ansgar urged his fellow monks to put aside their work on illuminated copies of the Bible and other famous books. "We must produce something that will sell, that will raise funds in this terrible time of poverty among the peasants and austerity among the gentry. Suppose, well … suppose we make pages that even the poor can buy. Let us make, well, say, copies of the Lord's Prayer."

And so they did—and the copies sold very well. But some of the brothers were not happy copying so many copies of the same thing. They wanted to be creative, inventive, imaginative. "Why not," said Brother Hypolitus, "do a paraphrase? Better yet, isn't it possible to improve upon this sentimental language? After all, to speak of God as 'Father' is to bring the holy into the profane. Why not speak of Him as 'Master' or 'Monarch' or 'Majesty?' Surely that will put the proper tone on the tongues of the rabble as they pray."

Poor Brother Ansgar. As much as he endeavored to retain the familiar address of the Lord's Prayer, his voice was too feeble. But his hands were agile. While the other brothers turned out one or two, possibly even three, copies of the Lord's Prayer a week, Brother Ansgar made that many in a day. He prayed as he painted, and painted as he conversed with God. But he could not write "Our Master" or "Our Monarch" or even "Our Majesty."

Brother Willigis was shocked. Brother Hypolitus was enraged.

"You have gone against the order," they rattled. "You have denied the authority of the abbot. Are you to make your own rules and ignore those of the order?"

"Well," said the fragile voice of the hoary-headed monk, "it is the *Lord's* prayer, and I think it should be left the way He gave it. God is our *Father.*"

"It's a matter of translation," said Brother Hypolitus, gesturing with a broad swish of his tiny hand in the immense sleeve of the coarse weave of his habit. "As far as I'm concerned, 'Father' is far too intimate a term; but 'Master' or 'Majesty' or 'Monarch,' well, they have a certain ring to them, a certain tone that should make men grovel rather than dance on God's knee."

"But God wants His children to sit on His knee," said Ansgar's creaking voice. At that, the brothers were offended. They reminded their elder brother that he must not speak so intimately of the Deity. Ansgar would have sins to pay and penalties for which to atone if he did not mind his arrogant ways.

It was Brother Kegley, the rotund keeper of the

monastery's accounts, who startled the order at one of their chapter meetings by announcing they had a huge inventory of "improved editions" (as they liked to call them) of the Lord's Prayer, but they were unable to keep in stock the traditional versions that only Brother Ansgar produced.

There was a bit of a hubbub and some snide remarks—then the clap of hands by the abbot. "Brothers, brothers," he remonstrated. "We must not quarrel, but instead tackle this new problem with Solomonic wit. I therefore decree that, henceforth and forevermore, there shall no longer be reproduced traditional copies. Only the improved editions are authorized; only they may be sold. That will take care of having too much stock. You, Brother Ansgar, have created a marketing dilemma that has caused us pain. Henceforth, you shall desist. In fact, you must leave the scriptorium for a season and assist the new priest in town. That should purify your soul."

Although the monks produced copy after copy of the new version, they did not sell. The shops refused to buy more. The monks' own stall at the county fair was ignored by the crowds, who mumbled that they had already a master in the palace who was not all that kind. They preferred God as a caring Father.

Brother Hypolitus was fuming with indignation. Brother Willigis tried to find words to refute the customers' requests for the traditional version, and Brother Kegley became more and more insistent that the monks push sales. "Discount them 10%," he ordered, and then 15%, even 25%. Finally the abbot made another Solomonic judgment: all would be reduced 50%.

The obstinate peasants responded, "We will pay twice the price for the traditional version, but nothing for these." Even the lords and ladies attending the fair would have nothing to do with the marked-down prayers.

Curiously, someone noted that, somehow, the atmosphere of the small villages near the mountain-top monastery changed. Indifferent neighbors were now good friends. Warring merchants who had previously tried to undercut other businessmen suddenly discovered prosperity was in cooperation rather than enmity. Brother Willigis was the first to notice it. He whispered it to Brother Kegley, who said something about it to Brother Hypolitus, who just happened to drop a hint or two about it to the abbot. "It must be the warmth of spring or the approach of summer," mumbled the abbot. "I can't determine which."

It was something else, however. It was Brother Ansgar.

Forbidden to illuminate manuscripts, Ansgar had to teach the children in the town church and ready youngsters for their First Communion. He prepared others for confirmation. And for the children in the orphanage, he was their mentor to help them learn their letters and to add two-and-two.

If Brother Ansgar was prohibited from making copies of the Lord's Prayer for the residents to buy, then he would be a living version for them to read. As the peasants saw Brother Ansgar lift children to his lap and tenderly share with them more than sums and letters, they saw a man of might whose power was in the compassion of his heart. They saw him ladle soup for the hungry and provide clothing for those in tattered outfits. They watched him treat the brothers of the order with kindly forgiveness, although they seemed to ridicule their elder. They saw him pray and heard his praise of God. They watched him and noticed that Brother Ansgar was a living copy of a living prayer. "Don't pray it by rote," he said to his students. "That's for the classroom. Pray it by thinking of the meaning, and mean it by the living of it."

How Brother Kegley, round as a barrel and plodding as a plow horse, discovered the change in the community was simply a matter of arithmetic. The empty coffers of the destitute monastery were being filled with gifts, small and large. They came in without a campaign. It was not due to sales and certainly not due to the drastic discount the abbot had ordered. It was that one man applied to life a prayer he fervently prayed. Suddenly the people there discovered the true family to which they belonged, and there was gaiety in rejoining the family circle.

And Brother Ansgar?

He decided that the art of living the Lord's Prayer is far more important than the art of illuminating the Lord's Prayer. To that the abbot agreed.

The old monastery is a museum today, but the tourists who wander through marvel at the one remaining illuminated copy of the Lord's Prayer Brother Ansgar made centuries before. With magnifying glass in hand, they examine the artful curlicues and golden ornamentations to discover a bit of advice. In the Latin of the

127

church of that time as well as in the local language, Brother Ansgar wrote, "We are all children … His children … who are a family with a dear Father and a saving Brother."

In this family, we pray …

Our Father: Praying, confessing, and living the Lord's Prayer go together. To confess it, one must live it; yet to live it, one must pray it—and pray it with a depth of faith that believes that the heavenly Father is truly *Abba*, the intimate and loving Father, who not only fathers offspring but cares for them, so there is neither an end to His love nor an end to our association with Him. Here is the key to confessing the Lord's Prayer: having that intimacy of faith that adores God because He is truly "*Abba* Father."

Who art in heaven: He is God enough to truly reside in heaven, but *Abba* enough to embrace His earthly family by sending His Son to live among them. He is our Creator, but He is also our *Abba* Father, for His Son was sent to the whole world.

Hallowed be Thy name: This Creator has a name honorable enough for every child, for every aging soul, and for everyone in between to respect as sacred and revere as holy, yet *Abba* enough to be more than familiar. He is so dear and close that even to speak His name with childlike abandon does not insult or offend Him, because our Savior and brother is His Son.

Thy kingdom come: He is God enough to command a kingdom, yet *Abba* enough to make us members of it and to send His Spirit within us, though none of us deserve His presence. He truly is our king, who has made us princes and princesses, earthlings with citizenship in heaven, commoners with an uncommon Father.

Thy will be done on earth as it is in heaven: He is God enough to subdue the earth as well as rule heaven, yet *Abba* enough to be merciful to scalawags and compassionate to those who are testy in their afflictions and arrogant in their self-sufficiency. He is God enough to will peace for His children, yet *Abba* enough to draw them together and reconcile their differences when they war with each other.

Give us this day our daily bread: He is God enough to feed and clothe His family, yet *Abba* enough to comfort us in our sorrow and crown us in our joys, to shelter us in the heat of summer and the cold of winter, to nourish us in our hunger and clothe us in our nakedness.

And forgive us our trespasses, as we forgive those who trespass against us: Above all, He is God enough to have standards, yet *Abba* enough to forgive us because of Jesus, to amend our waywardness with His understanding, and to atone for our disobedience through His own sacrifice; for, in our helplessness, we cannot atone for ourselves.

129

Lead us not into temptation: He most assuredly is God enough to save us from the distresses of life and the persecutions faith brings, but *Abba* enough never to abandon us, despite the plights of this planet. He is God enough to stay hands that would obliterate us, but *Abba* enough to teach cruel hands tender neighborliness.

But deliver us from evil: He is God enough to be watchful of us, yet *Abba* enough to help us learn from little mistakes so that we hesitate from engaging in larger blunders. He is God enough to punish the source of evil, but *Abba* enough to see beyond evil's infection to give us hope and assurances, to love us out of defeat into Christ's victory.

For Thine is the kingdom and the power and the glory forever and ever: To live the spirit of the Lord's Prayer is to expect God to make us an answer to the petitions. So we praise God by being a doxology ourselves to the stranger and the friend, to the neighbor and the enemy, giving Him glory by a prayer prayed, a creed confessed, and a life lived.

It is an endless circle of joy, this praying the prayer He taught us and confessing the ideas He gave us, for the two actions nurture each other in Christ. He is the one who bridges the sacred and the profane with His incarnation. He is the one who made the cross a symbol of conquest rather than a lurid emblem of ruin. He made life out of death and turned sorrow into joy. In this way

Jesus leads us in confessing the Lord's Prayer, and we follow Him by transforming words into action.

Only when the Lord leads us does the praying of the prayer become more than the saying of words, and the living of it celebrates the God who is God, yet truly our Father and most definitely our *Abba*. At that moment our hearts break loose into singing, and praise is not only heard upon our lips but confessed in our actions, for Jesus Christ has come and given us a prayer.

Notes

Introduction

1. William Barclay, *The Gospel of Matthew*, vol. 1 (Philadelphia: Westminster, 1975), 199; *Encyclopedia Britannica*, vol. 14 (1970), 311; and Martin Luther, *The Large Catechism*, tr. John Nicholas Lenker (Minneapolis: Augsburg, 1935), 112.

2. Selma Lagerlöf, *The Story of Gösta Berling* (Garden City, NY: Doubleday, Page & Company, 1925), 4–7.

3. William Temple, *Selections from the Writings of William Temple*, arr. and ed. Sulon G. Ferree (Nashville: The Upper Room, 1968), 19–20.

4. Martin Luther, "The Lord's Prayer," in "The Large Catechism," par. 52, in *The Book of Concord*, tr. Theodore G. Tappert (Philadelphia: Muhlenberg), 427.

5. Jan Milic Lochman, *The Lord's Prayer* (Grand Rapids: Eerdmans, 1990), 5.

Our Father

1. Thielicke's theology is discussed by Herbert Girgensohn, *Teaching Luther's Catechism* (Philadelphia: Muhlenberg, 1959), 203.

2. Thomas Watson, *The Lord's Prayer* (Edinburgh: The Banner of Truth Trust, 1982), 3.

3. Lochman, *The Lord's Prayer*, 19.

4. Barclay, *The Gospel of Matthew*, 203.

5. Vernon R. Schreiber, *Abba! Father!* (Minneapolis: Augsburg, 1988), 27.

6. Leonhard Ragaz, "Das Unservater," in *Von Der Revolution der Bible* (Zurich: 1943) 1:9, paraphrased by Lochman, *The Lord's Prayer*, 24.

Who Art in Heaven

1. Samuel Becket, *Waiting for Godot* (New York: Grove Weidenfeld, 1954), 61.

2. Walter A. Maier, *He Will Abundantly Pardon* (St. Louis: Concordia, 1948), 2.

3. This translation of the creed is from *Lutheran Book of Worship* (Minneapolis: Augsburg, 1978) 64.

4. Martin Luther, "A Simple Way to Pray," in *Luther's Works,* vol. 43 (Philadelphia: Fortress, 1968), 193–94.

5. Fannie Flagg, *Fried Green Tomatoes at the Whistle Stop Cafe* (New York: McGraw-Hill, 1988), 325.

6. Everett L. Fullam, *Living the Lord's Prayer* (Grand Rapids: Zondervan, 1980), 37.

Hallowed Be Thy Name

1. Malcolm Muggeridge, *Confessions of a Twentieth-Century Pilgrim* (San Francisco: Harper & Row, 1988), 24.

2. Fullam, *Living the Lord's Prayer*, 48.

3. Curtis C. Mitchell, *Praying Jesus' Way* (Tarrytown, NY: Revell, 1991), 46.

4. Selma Lagerlöf, *The Ring of the Lowenskjölds* (New York: Literary Guild, 1931), 19.

Thy Kingdom Come

1. John Fante, *Ask the Dust* (Santa Rosa: Black Sparrow Press, 1980), 22.

2. Irenaeus, "Against Heresies," *The Ante-Nicene Fathers,* vol. 1 (Grand Rapids: Eerdmans, n. d.) 5.32–33; Watson, *The Lord's Prayer,* 59; Fullam, *Living the Lord's Prayer,* 68; Walter Rauschenbusch, *A Theology for the Social Gospel* (Nashville: Abingdon, 1981), 47; Bonhoeffer, "Dein Reich komme," *Gesammelte Schriften,* as quoted by Lochman, *The Lord's Prayer,* 45–48; Girgensohn, *Teaching Luther's Catechism,* 243–44; Karl H. Hertz, "Kingdom of God," in *The Encyclopedia of the Lutheran Church* (Minneapolis: Augsburg, 1965), 1214; Kurt Rommel, *Our Father Who Art in Heaven* (Philadelphia: Fortress, 1981), 31; Barclay, *The Gospel of Matthew,* 211; John Bright, *The Kingdom of God* (Nashville: Abingdon, 1953), 244; Luther, "The Large Catechism," *The Book of Concord,* par. 351–52, pp. 426–27; Helmut Thielicke, *The Waiting Father* (New York: Harper & Row, 1959), 183; and Thielicke, *Our Heavenly Father* (New York: Harper & Row, 1960), 47.

3. C. S. Lewis, *Letters to Malcolm: Chiefly on Prayer* (New York: Harcourt Brace Jovanovich, 1964), 24–25.

4. E. M. Blaiklock, *The Positive Power of Prayer* (Glendale, CA: Regal Books, 1974), 29.

5. Mitchell, *Praying Jesus' Way,* 46.

6. Carl E. Braaten, *Stewards of the Mysteries* (Minneapolis: Augsburg, 1983), 38.

Thy Will Be Done on Earth as It Is in Heaven

1. Dr. Billy Graham, *Answers to Life's Problems* (Dallas: Word, 1988), 174; Girgensohn, *Teaching Luther's Catechism,* 257; Muggeridge, *Confessions of a Twentieth-Century Pilgrim,* Foreword; and C. S. Lewis, *Letters to Malcolm,* 25–26.

2. Nathan Söderblom, "Continued Revelation," from his Gifford Lectures, in *The World Treasury of Modern Religious Thought,* Pelikan, Jaroslav, ed. (Boston: Little, Brown, 1990), 277.

3. James L. Adams, *Yankee Doodle Went to Church* (Old Tappan, NJ: Revell, 1989), 197.

4. John Eidsmoe, "Overwhelming Majority of Founding Fathers Were Christian, Not Godless or Deist," *American Family Association Journal* (July 1989), 22.

5. W. B. J. Martin, *Sermons for Special Days* (Nashville: Abingdon, 1975), 94.

6. Adams, *Yankee Doodle Went to Church,* 94.

7. Patrick J. Buchanan, "The War for the Soul of America," in *American Family Association Journal* (published by the AFA, July 1992), 15.

8. Adams, *Yankee Doodle Went to Church,* 161–62.

Give Us This Day Our Daily Bread

1. Mark Twain, *The Prince and the Pauper* (New York: Bantam Books, 1982), 9, 12.

2. Thomas á Kempis, *The Imitation of Christ,* Douglas V. Stere, ed. (Nashville: The Upper Room, 1950), 22.

3. Fullam, *Living the Lord's Prayer,* 86.

4. Martin Luther, *The Small Catechism* (Minneapolis: Augsburg, 1979), 20.

5. Lochman, *The Lord's Prayer,* pp. 85, 89–90; and Barclay, *The Gospel of Matthew,* 215.

6. James Kallas, *Jesus and the Power of Satan* (Philadelphia: Westminster, 1958), 146–47.

7. Alexander Solzhenitsyn, *One Day in the Life of Ivan Denisovich* (New York: New American Library—Dutton, 1963), 153–54.

8. R. C. Sproul, *Effective Prayer* (Wheaton: Tyndale, 1989), 35.

9. Blaiklock, *The Positive Power of Prayer,* 35

10. Fullam, *Living the Lord's Prayer*, 92; and Lochman, *The Lord's Prayer*, 90–91.

11. Barclay, *The Gospel of Matthew*, 218.

12. Steve Harper, *Praying Through the Lord's Prayer* (Nashville: The Upper Room, 1992), 74.

Forgive Us Our Trespasses as We Forgive Those Who Trespass against Us

1. Charles Dickens, *A Tale of Two Cities* (New York: Penguin Books, 1980), 353.

2. C. S. Lewis, *Letters to Malcolm*, 27.

3. Martin Luther, "The Sermon on the Mount," in *Luther's Works*, vol. 21 (St. Louis: Concordia, 1956), 98.

4. Ron Lee Davis, *A Forgiving God in an Unforgiving World* (Eugene, OR: Harvest House, 1984), 61–62.

5. Paul Tournier, *Creative Suffering* (San Francisco: Harper & Row, 1981), 99–100.

6. Paul Tillich, *The New Being* (New York: Scribners, 1955), 8, 10.

7. Luther, *The Large Catechism* (1935), 150–51; and Alvin N. Rogness, *Forgiveness and Confession* (Minneapolis: Augsburg, 1970), 34.

8. Watson, *The Lord's Prayer*, 209.

Lead Us Not into Temptation, but Deliver Us from Evil

1. Gerald Kennedy, *Fresh Every Morning* (New York: Harper & Row, 1966), 99.

2. Kenneth Leech, *True Prayer* (San Francisco: Harper & Row, 1980), 145; and Barclay, *The Gospel of Matthew*, 224.

3. Norman Victor Hope, ed., *Selections from the Writings of John Knox* (Nashville: The Upper Room, 1957), 10.

4. Nien Cheng, *Life and Death in Shanghai* (New York: Grove Press, 1986), 346–47.

5. Solzhenitsyn, *Ivan Denisovich*, 153.

6. Pavel Uhorskai, *Uncompromising Faith* (St. Louis: Concordia, 1992), 67.

7. Philip Yancey, *Praying With the KGB* (Portland: Multnomah, 1992), 39–48.

8. Fullam, *Living the Lord's Prayer*, 113.

9. D. Martyn Lloyd-Jones, *Faith on Trial* (Grand Rapids: Eerdmans, 1965), 101.

10. Ibid., 97.

Thine Is the Kingdom and the Power and the Glory Forever and Ever. Amen.

1. Fullam, *Living the Lord's Prayer*, 127.

2. Girgensohn, *Teaching Luther's Catechism*, 302; and Luther D. Reed, *The Lutheran Liturgy* (Philadelphia: Muhlenberg, 1947), 252.

3. "The Teaching of the Twelve Apostles," VIII:2, in *The Ante-Nicene Fathers*, vol. 7, 379.

4. C. S. Lewis, *Letters to Malcolm*, 28.

5. Luther, *The Small Catechism* (1979), 22.

6. W. E. Vine, Merrill F. Unger, and William White, eds., *An Expository Dictionary of Biblical Words*, New Testament (Nashville: Thomas Nelson, 1985), 25.

7. Jane Stuart Smith and Betty Carlson, *A Gift of Music* (Westchester, IL: Good News Publishers, 1978), 68.

8. Lochman, *The Lord's Prayer*, 163.

9. Peter Marshall, "Praying is Dangerous Business," a sermon included in Catherine Marshall's biography of her husband, *A Man Called Peter* (New York: McGraw-Hill, 1951), 321–22.

10. Information from a brochure published by the Walter Inglis Anderson Museum, Ocean Springs, MS, designed by Jim Edminson (1991).

Bibliography

Adams, James L. *Yankee Doodle Went to Church.* Old Tappan, NJ: Revell, 1989.

Barclay, William. *The Gospel of Matthew,* vol. 1. Philadelphia: Westminster, 1975.

Becket, Samuel. *Waiting for Godot.* New York: Grove Weidenfeld, 1954.

Blaiklock, E. M. *The Positive Power of Prayer.* Glendale, CA: Regal Books, 1974.

Braaten, Carl E. *Stewards of the Mysteries.* Minneapolis: Augsburg, 1983.

Bright, John. *The Kingdom of God.* Nashville: Abingdon, 1953.

Buchanan, Patrick J. "The War for the Soul of America." *American Family Association Journal* (July 1992): 15.

Cheng, Nien. *Life and Death in Shanghai.* New York: Grove Press, 1987.

Davis, Ron Lee. *A Forgiving God in an Unforgiving World.* Eugene, OR: Harvest House, 1984.

Dickens, Charles. *A Tale of Two Cities.* New York: Penguin Books, 1980.

Eidsmoe, John. "Overwhelming Majority of Founding Fathers Were Christian, Not Godless or Deist." *American Family Association Journal* (July 1989): 22.

Fante, John. *Ask the Dust.* Santa Rosa: Black Sparrow Press, 1980.

Flagg, Fannie. *Fried Green Tomatoes at the Whistle Stop Cafe.* New York: McGraw-Hill, 1988.

Fullam, Everett L. *Living the Lord's Prayer.* Grand Rapids: Zondervan, 1980.

Girgensohn, Herbert. *Teaching Luther's Catechism.* Philadelphia: Muhlenberg, 1959.

Graham, Dr. Billy. *Answers to Life's Problems.* Dallas: Word, 1988.

Harper, Steve. *Praying Through the Lord's Prayer.* Nashville: The Upper Room, 1992.

Hertz, Karl H. "Kingdom of God." In *The Encyclopedia of the Lutheran Church,* 1213–14. Minneapolis: Augsburg, 1965.

Hope, Norman Victor, ed. *Selections from the Writings of John Knox.* Nashville: The Upper Room, 1957.

Irenaeus, "Against Heresies." In *The Ante-Nicene Fathers,* vol. 1, 309–567, American Reprint of the Edinburgh Edition. Grand Rapids: Eerdmans, n.d.

Kallas, James. *Jesus and the Power of Satan.* Philadelphia: Westminster, 1958.

Kennedy, Gerald. *Fresh Every Morning.* New York: Harper & Row, 1966.

Lagerlöf, Selma. *The Story of Gösta Berling.* Garden City, NY: Doubleday, Page & Company, 1925.

_____. *The Ring of the Lowenskjölds.* New York: Literary Guild, 1931.

Leech, Kenneth; *True Prayer.* San Francisco: Harper & Row, 1980.

Lewis, C. S. *Letters to Malcolm: Chiefly on Prayer.* New York: Harcourt Brace Jovanovich, 1973.

Lloyd-Jones, D. Martyn. *Faith on Trial.* Grand Rapids: Eerdmans, 1965.

Lochman, Jan Milic. *The Lord's Prayer.* Grand Rapids: Wm. B. Eerdmans, 1990.

Luther, Martin. *The Large Catechism.* Luther material translated by John Nicholas Lenker. Minneapolis: Augsburg, 1935.

_____. "The Lord's Prayer." In "The Large Catechism," *The Book of Concord,* translated by Theodore G. Tappert. Philadelphia: Muhlenberg, 1959.

_____. "The Sermon on the Mount." Translated by Jaroslav Pelikan. In *Luther's Works,* vol. 21. St. Louis: Concordia: 1956.

_____. "A Simple Way to Pray." Translated by Carl J. Schindler. In *Luther's Works,* vol. 43 Philadelphia: Fortress, 1968.

_____. *The Small Catechism.* Minneapolis: Augsburg, 1979.

Lutheran Book of Worship. Minneapolis: Augsburg, 1978.

Maier, Walter A. *He Will Abundantly Pardon.* St. Louis: Concordia, 1948.

Marshall, Peter. "Praying Is Dangerous Business." In *A Man Called Peter,* Catherine Marshall. New York: McGraw-Hill, 1951.

Martin, W. B. J. *Sermons for Special Days.* Nashville: Abingdon, 1975.

Mitchell, Curtis C. *Praying Jesus' Way.* Tarrytown, NY: Revell, 1991.

Muggeridge, Malcolm. *Confessions of a Twentieth-Century Pilgrim.* San Francisco: Harper & Row, 1988.

Neuhaus, Richard John. *The Naked Public Square.* Grand Rapids: Eerdmans, 1984.

Rauschenbusch, Walter. *A Theology for the Social Gospel.* Reprint. Nashville: Abingdon, 1981.

Reed, Luther D. *The Lutheran Liturgy.* Philadelphia: Muhlenberg, 1947.

Rogness, Alvin N. *Forgiveness and Confession.* Minneapolis: Augsburg, 1970.

Rommel, Kurt. *Our Father Who Art in Heaven.* Philadelphia: Fortress, 1981.

Schreiber, Vernon R. *Abba! Father!* Minneapolis: Augsburg, 1988.

Smith, Jane Stuart, and Betty Carlson. *A Gift of Music.* Westchester, IL: Good News Publishers, 1978.

Söderblom, Nathan. "Continued Revelation." Excerpt from his Gifford Lectures. In *The World Treasury of Modern Religious Thought,* Pelikan, Jaroslav, ed. Boston: Little, Brown, 1990.

Solzhenitsyn, Alexander. *One Day in the Life of Ivan Denisovich.* New York: New American Library—Dutton, 1963.

Sproul, R. C. *Effective Prayer.* Wheaton: Tyndale, 1989.

"The Teaching of the Twelve Apostles." In *The Ante-Nicene Fathers,* vol. 7, 377–82. American Reprint of the Edinburgh Edition. Grand Rapids: Eerdmans, n.d.

Temple, William. *Selections from the Writings of William Temple.* Arranged and edited by Sulon G. Ferree. Nashville: The Upper Room, 1968.

Thielicke, Helmut. *Our Heavenly Father*. New York: Harper & Row, 1960.

_____. *The Waiting Father*. New York: Harper & Row, 1959.

Thomas á Kempis, *The Imitation of Christ*. Douglas V. Stere, ed. Nashville: The Upper Room, 1950.

Tillich, Paul. *The New Being*. New York: Scribners, 1955.

Tournier, Paul. *Creative Suffering*. San Francisco: Harper & Row, 1981.

Twain, Mark. *The Prince and the Pauper*. New York: Bantam Books, 1982.

Uhorskai, Pavel. *Uncompromising Faith*. St. Louis: Concordia, 1992.

Vine, W. E., Merrill F. Unger, and William White, eds. *An Expository Dictionary of Biblical Words*. Nashville: Thomas Nelson Publishers, 1985.

Watson, Thomas. *The Lord's Prayer*. Edinburgh: The Banner of Truth Trust, 1982.

Yancey, Philip. *Praying with the KGB*. Portland: Multnomah, 1992.